ACT Therapy Workbook for Kids

Fun Guided Activities for Mindfulness, Compassion, and Empathy with Acceptance & Commitment Therapy

Help Children Ages 8-12 Manage Anxiety, Worry, Anger, Sadness & More

By Barrett Huang
https://barretthuang.com/

© Copyright 2024 by Barrett Huang. All rights reserved.

This book contains information that is as accurate and reliable as possible. Regardless, purchasing this book constitutes an agreement that both the publisher and the author are in no way experts on the topics discussed and that any comments or suggestions made herein are solely for educational purposes. The information provided is not a substitute for professional medical advice, diagnosis, or treatment. Always consult a professional before taking any action advised herein.

This declaration is deemed fair and valid by both the American Bar Association and the Committee of Publishers Association and is legally binding throughout the United States.

Furthermore, the transmission, duplication, or reproduction of any of the following work, including specific information, will be considered illegal, whether done electronically or in print. This extends to creating a secondary or tertiary copy of the work or a recorded copy and is only allowed with express written consent from the publisher. All additional rights reserved.

The information in the following pages is broadly considered a truthful and accurate account of facts. Any inattention, use, or misuse of the information in question by the reader will render any resulting actions solely under their purview. There are no scenarios in which the publisher or author of this work can be deemed liable for any hardship or damages that may occur after undertaking the information described herein.

Additionally, the information in the following pages is intended only for informational purposes. It should thus be thought of as universal. It is presented without assurance regarding its prolonged validity or interim quality as befitting its nature. Trademarks mentioned are done without written consent and should not be considered an endorsement from the trademark holder.

Cover Attribution Page

Cover Attribution:

Cover image by Freepik from <u>Freepik</u>.

FREE GUIDE: Mental Health Boosters for Kids

FREE DOWNLOAD ALERT!

Fun and Engaging Activities to Manage Your Children's Emotional Well-Being

https://barretthuang.com/mental-health-boosters/

Or scan the code below:

Contents

Cover Attribution Page..3

FREE GUIDE: Mental Health Boosters for Kids.................................4

Introduction..8

Dear Parents:..8

    What is ACT?...8

    How You Can Support Your Child...9

Understanding Your Feelings..21

What Are Feelings?...32

    Fun Activity #1: Today I Feel..34

    Fun Activity #2: Feelings Diary...35

    Fun Activity #3: Safe People..38

    Fun Activity #4: Feelings and Body Map...................................40

What Mindfulness Means..45

What Is Mindfulness?...56

    Fun Activity #5: Mindful Breathing..58

    Fun Activity #6: Mindful Listening...59

    Fun Activity #7: Mindful Eating...61

    Fun Activity #8: Mindfulness Jar...63

    Fun Activity #9: Mindful Coloring..65

Acceptance and Letting Go..69

What Is Acceptance?...78

What is "Letting Go"? 78

Why It's Sometimes Important to NOT Act on Our Feelings 78

Fun Activity #10: Balloon Release 79

Fun Activity #11: The Worry Box 82

Fun Activity #12: I'm a Good Kid 84

Learning About Your Thoughts 89

What Are Thoughts? 104

Understanding Thoughts vs. Reality 105

Fun Activity #13: Thought Bubbles 106

Fun Activity #14: Thought Train 111

You are NOT Your Thoughts 112

Fun Activity #15: Clouds in the Sky 114

Fun Activity #16: Mountain Meditation 116

Fun Activity #17: Thought Untangling Cards 118

Knowing What Matters 121

What Are Values? 130

Fun Activity #18: Values BINGO 132

Fun Activity #19: Likes and Dislikes 135

Fun Activity #20: It's My Birthday! It's My Birthday! 138

Doing What Matters 141

What "Doing What Matters" Mean 148

Fun Activity #21: Doing What Matters Schedule 149

Fun Activity #22: I'm a SMART Kid 152

Fun Activity #23: W.O.O.P. Your Goal! 156

Fun Activity #24: Values Success Scrapbook 158

Kindness, Compassion, and Empathy 161

What is Kindness and Compassion? 170

    What's Empathy? 170

    Fun Activity #25: Kindness Game Board 172

    Fun Activity #26: Amazing Friendships 177

    Fun Activity #27: Patience, Patience 179

Staying Healthy and Happy 181

How to Develop Good Habits to Be Amazing Kids 196

    Fun Activity #28: High Five to Healthy Habits 197

    Fun Activity #29: Writing a Letter to a Friend or Family Member 200

    Fun Activity #30: No-Screen Fun Stuff 204

Conclusion 207

Review Request 215

Further Reading 216

About the Author 219

Introduction

Dear Parents:

Welcome to "ACT for Kids"! We are thrilled that you are interested in learning about Acceptance and Commitment Therapy (ACT) and how it can support your child's emotional well-being.

What is ACT?

ACT stands for Acceptance and Commitment Therapy. It is a therapy that helps people, including children, deal with their feelings and thoughts healthily. You might be thinking, "My child does not need therapy." That may be true, but one is never too young to learn how to effectively handle emotions and negative self-beliefs, right?

The earlier kids learn to understand and manage unhelpful feelings and thoughts, the stronger their self-confidence will become, positively impacting how they navigate their teenage years and adulthood.

ACT teaches children to accept their emotions rather than fight them—even if they are difficult. It also teaches them how to detach from negative self-beliefs such as "Nobody likes me at school," "I can't do it," "I just suck at stuff," and more. Lastly, ACT teaches kids how to behave in alignment with positive values such as respect, honesty, responsibility, and more.

ACT is based on six core principles to help your child navigate their emotions and experiences: *Acceptance, Mindfulness, Cognitive Defusion, Self-as-Context, Values Clarification,* and *Committed Action.*

Yes, these six principles are quite BIG words, but do not worry! This workbook will drastically simplify these concepts using language that kids will understand.

Additionally, to make learning about ACT fun and engaging, your child will be guided by **Tibby & Zip**—the world's favorite sibling kitties! 🐾

Each chapter begins with a short and captivating story featuring Tibby & Zip to spark your child's interest in ACT. As they follow along with the stories and complete the exercises, they will naturally absorb ACT principles, making the learning process enjoyable and effective. Sounds fun already, right?

How You Can Support Your Child

We have designed this book to be kid-friendly, but your support is crucial on this journey. To help you guide your child effectively, please download our free bonus, "**Mental Health Boosters for Kids**." This resource will give you additional tips and strategies to help your child through their self-improvement journey.

Now, let's get your kids started!

Hi there! I am Tibby, and this is my younger brother Zip. We live in Kittyville with our mom and dad. We love playing outdoors, eating fish snacks, and chasing butterflies!

We are so excited you are here to join us on this ACT adventure! Before we start, do you want to share something about yourself, too? We would love to get to know you.

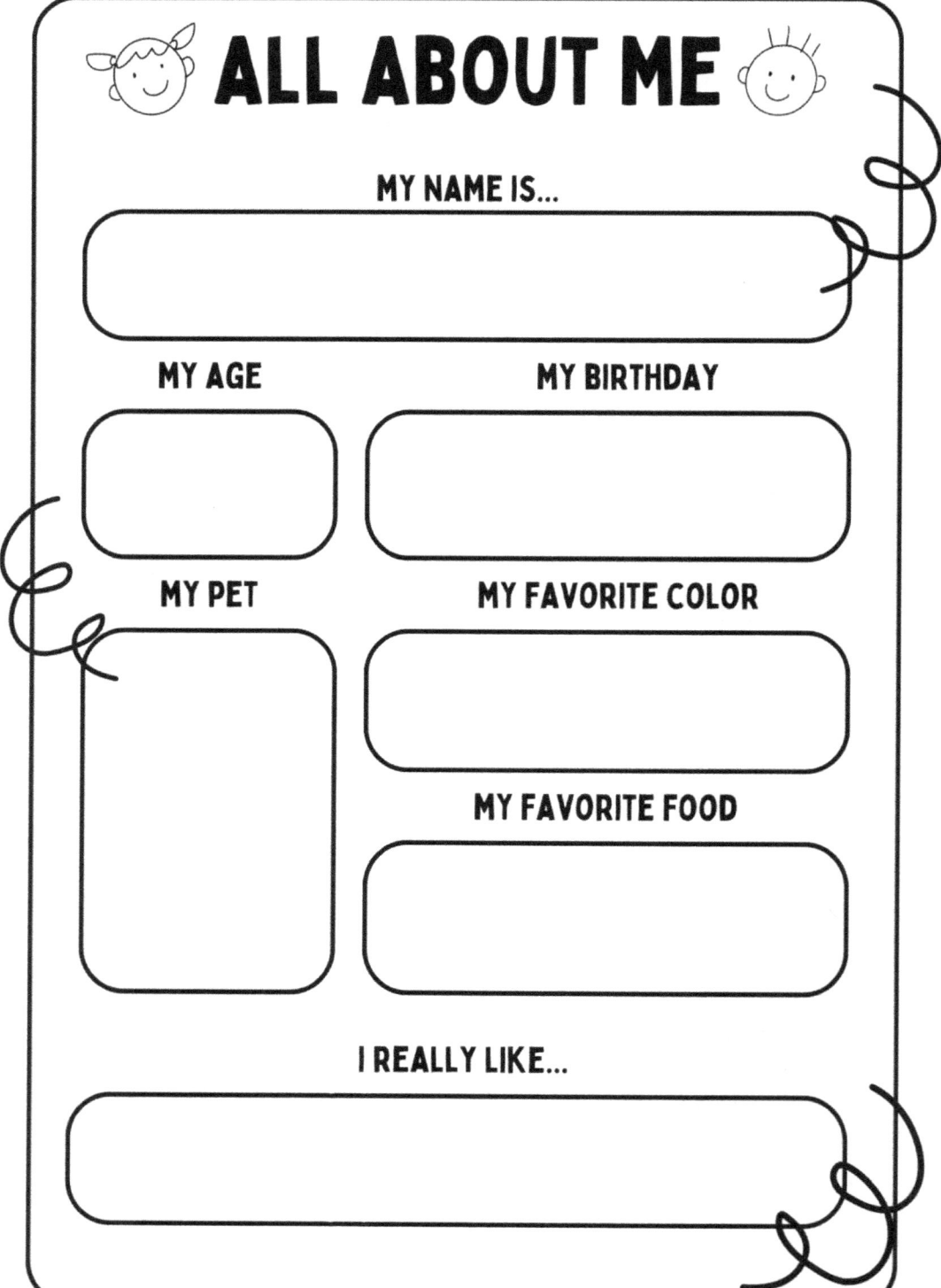

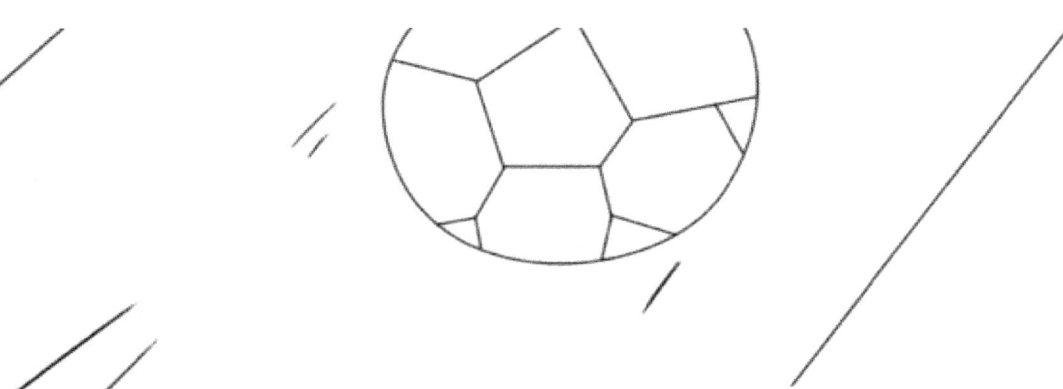

Oh! Zip and I have a question. (Sorry, we are nosy kitties!) Have you ever felt super happy one moment and then really sad or angry next? You know, that is totally normal. We all have different feelings, and it is okay to feel ALL of them.

That is actually what this adventure is all about. It will help you better understand your feelings and thoughts using this super cool thing called Acceptance and Commitment Therapy (ACT). Do not worry if that sounds weird. We will make sure ACT is easy and fun for you, okay?

But first, let me share why Zip and I love ACT.

It helps you feel better when you are upset.
It makes focusing on fun, happiness, and important things easier.
It helps you make good choices based on what you like or feel is important.

We promise you are going to have lots of fun learning about ACT. We will share stories, play games, and do cool activities with you.

Are you ready to start this adventure? Let's go!

Your furry friends,
Tibby & Zip

Understanding Your Feelings

Chapter 1: Understanding Your Feelings

One sunny morning in Kittyville, Tibby and Zip were playing outside. They love to explore their garden, which is filled with colorful flowers and buzzing bees. Zip suddenly notices a shiny red ball under a bush. He pounced on it excitedly, but as he did, a big, scary shadow moved across the ground, and Zip froze in fear!

"What is wrong, Zip?" Tibby asked, noticing her brother's frightened face.

"I saw a shadow, Tibby! It scared me."

Tibby gave Zip a comforting nuzzle. "It's okay to feel scared, Zip. Everyone feels different emotions. Sometimes we are happy, sometimes we are sad, and sometimes we are scared. All these feelings are part of us."

Zip looked up at Tibby with wide eyes. "Really? Even you feel scared sometimes?"

"Of course," Tibby said with a gentle smile. "Understanding our feelings helps us know what to do with them. For example, when you get scared when you see the shadow, it is good to pause for a second. And then, you can remind yourself that shadows are just caused by the sun, and there is nothing to fear. It is just a part of understanding our feelings and knowing they come and go.'

"So, it is okay to feel scared,
but I do not have to stay scared?" Zip asked,
starting to feel better.

"Exactly!" Tibby replied. "Feelings are like the weather—they change. The more we understand them, the better we can handle them. Now, let's go check out that shadow together!"

With Tibby by his side, Zip felt braver.
They approached the bush and discovered that
the shadow was just from a large tree branch
swaying in the wind. Zip laughed in relief
and picked up the red ball."

"See, Zip? There was nothing to be scared of,"
Tibby said. "And now we can keep playing!"

What Are Feelings?

Feelings are the emotions we experience inside us. They help us understand how we feel about different things that happen to us. Everyone has feelings, and it is important to know that all feelings are okay to have.

But did you know that there are only seven basic feelings or emotions that humans experience? Here they are:

- **Happiness.** You might smile, laugh, or feel warm and excited inside when you feel happy. It happens when something good happens, like playing with friends or getting a hug from someone you like or love.

- **Sadness.** You might want to cry or feel quiet and low when you feel sad. It happens when something bad happens, like losing a toy or missing someone.

- **Anger.** You might feel hot and want to shout or stomp your feet when you feel angry. It happens when something feels unfair, or you do not get what you want.

- **Fear.** When you feel scared, you might want to hide or run away. It happens when something seems dangerous or unknown, like a loud noise or a big shadow.

- **Surprise.** When you are surprised, your eyes might open wide, and your mouth drop open. It happens when something unexpected happens, like a sudden gift, a surprise party, or a really loud noise you were not expecting.

- **Disgust.** When you feel disgusted, you might wrinkle your nose or feel like saying "yuck." It happens when you see or taste something unpleasant, like a bad smell or yucky food.

- **Interest.** When you feel interested, you might lean in closer and focus on something. It happens when you find something really cool or exciting, like a new game or a fun story.

You might think, "But I don't feel any of these seven emotions. I'm bored!" Ah, but you see, *bored* can come from feeling sad (because there is nothing to do!) or disinterest (because nothing seems exciting).

So, you see? One way or the other, your feelings will most likely come under one of the seven basic emotions above. (Kinda cool, huh?)

Just remember that all feelings are normal to have, and by understanding your feelings, you can learn how to handle them better, just like Tibby and Zip. Now, let's keep exploring more about feelings with the following fun activities!

Fun Activity #1: Today I Feel

What are you feeling today? Whatever it is, grab a crayon or colored pencil and start coloring the "emotion jar" that suits your feelings. For example, you might want to use the color "blue" if you're sad or the color "red" if you're angry. By giving your emotions a color, you will start to understand your feelings better.

Fun Activity #2: Feelings Diary

You did a GREAT JOB in recognizing your feelings in the previous activity. But did you know that you cannot feel the same thing all the time? So, let's make a Feelings Diary!

Keeping a diary helps you recognize and understand your feelings better. It will also help you express what is inside you.

So, for just one super short week, circle your feelings and why. Ready? Let's go!

Here's an example:

Monday: Today, I'm feeling:

| Happy | Scared | Sad | Surprised | Angry | Interested | Disgusted |

I feel <u>interested</u> because:

We have a new neighbor next door, and they have a cute baby. I wonder if I can visit and play with the baby sometime.

Okay, it's your turn now!

Monday: Today, I'm feeling:

| Happy | Scared | Sad | Surprised | Angry | Interested | Disgusted |

I feel _____ because:

_____

_____

_____

Tuesday: Today, I'm feeling:

| Happy | Scared | Sad | Surprised | Angry | Interested | Disgusted |

I feel _____ because:

_____

_____

_____

Wednesday: Today, I'm feeling:

| Happy | Scared | Sad | Surprised | Angry | Interested | Disgusted |

I feel _____ because:

_____

_____

_____

Thursday: Today, I'm feeling:

| Happy | Scared | Sad | Surprised | Angry | Interested | Disgusted |

I feel _____ because:

_____

_____

_____

Friday: Today, I'm feeling:

| Happy | Scared | Sad | Surprised | Angry | Interested | Disgusted |

I feel _____ because:

_____
_____
_____

Saturday: Today, I'm feeling:

| Happy | Scared | Sad | Surprised | Angry | Interested | Disgusted |

I feel _____ because:

_____
_____
_____

Sunday: Today, I'm feeling:

| Happy | Scared | Sad | Surprised | Angry | Interested | Disgusted |

I feel _____ because:

_____
_____
_____

GREAT JOB! You can make it a habit to write or draw in your Feelings Diary for longer than a week if you want. The more you practice, the better you will understand your emotions!

Fun Activity #3: Safe People

When you are very sad or angry or just not feeling okay at all, talking to an adult you trust helps. Just sharing your feelings, especially the not-so-happy ones, often helps you feel better.

But WHO do you talk to about your feelings? Great question!

How about you prepare now and think about the people who make you feel safe and happy. These are your "Safe People."

1.) Under each outline below, glue a picture of one of your Safe People. If you don't have a picture, just write their name on the outline. It could be your mom, dad, teacher, best friend, or anyone who makes you feel safe and loved.

2.) Use your crayons or markers to color each outline. Make them bright and colorful, just like the special people they represent!

3.) If you have more than three Safe People, that is awesome! Write their names down, too. You can even get another piece of paper to draw more Safe People outlines.

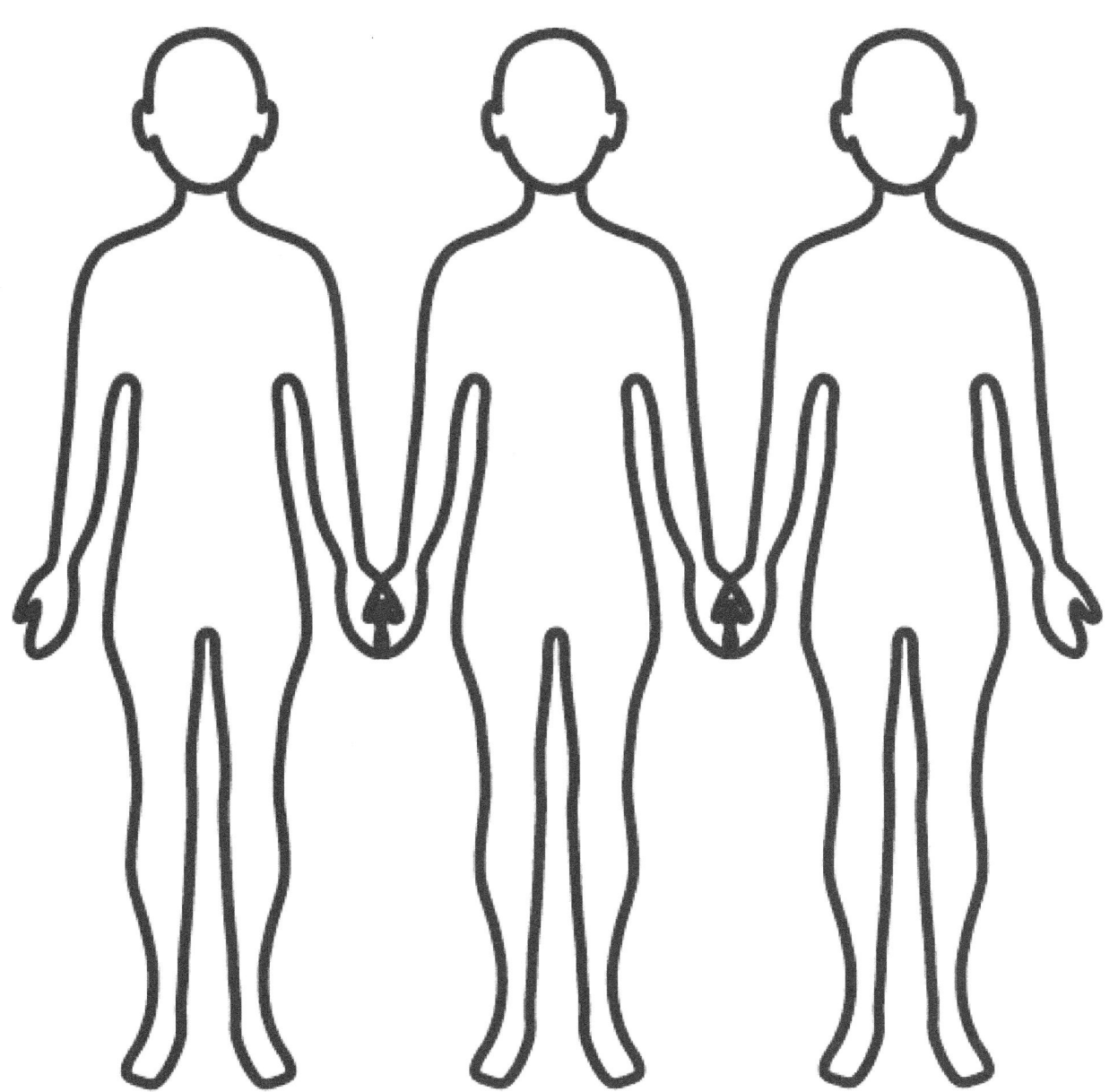

My Safe People are:

#1. _____

#2. _____

#3. _____

Fun Activity #4: Feelings and Body Map

Did you know that your feelings sometimes show up in your body? That is true! For example, when you are **worried** about something, you might get a headache or even a tummy ache.

Knowing how your feelings appear in your body helps you better understand yourself. And that is important because sometimes we do not have the words for what we feel; we just, you know, feel them in our bodies.

1.) Close your eyes for a moment and think about the different feelings you have had this week. How did your body feel when you were happy, sad, angry, scared, or excited?

2.) On the body outlines below, label different parts of your body where you feel emotions. Here are some ideas for you:

- **Head**: When you are happy, you might have happy thoughts floating in your mind. When you are worried or stressed, you might have a headache.

- **Eyes**: When you are sad, you might cry. When you are surprised, your eyes might be opened wide.

- **Mouth**: You might smile when you are happy or frown when you are sad.

- **Heart**: When you are happy, your heart may feel full or feel like there is a brightly shining sun inside it. When you are scared, your heart might beat fast.

- **Stomach**: You might feel butterflies in your stomach when you are nervous or upset.

- **Hands**: Your hands might feel shaky when you are anxious or closed into tight fists when you are angry.

These are just examples. Your body can feel and do many other things depending on your feelings.

3.) **Get out your crayons!** Use different colors to show how each feeling affects your body. For example:
- Use yellow to show happiness in your face and heart.
- Use blue to show sadness in your eyes and heart.
- Use red to show anger in your hands and face.
- Use green to show calmness in your stomach and heart.
- Use purple to show excitement in your heart and hands.

Use any color you like for whatever emotion. You are the boss!

4.) **Draw to your heart's content.** If you want to, draw or write more details about how each feeling affects your body. For example, you might want to draw a happy face near your head if you are happy or write "butterflies" near your stomach if you are scared or worried.

Okay then, pick the image you want for your Feelings and Body Map below.

What Mindfulness Means

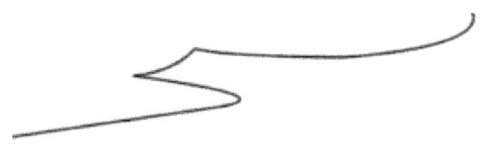

One beautiful morning, Tibby and Zip were at the park.
Tibby was sitting on a bench, enjoying the warm sun
and the soft sound of the wind rustling through the trees.
Full of energy, Zip ran up to her and said,
"Tibby, come on! Let's go play tag with the other kittens!"

Tibby opened her eyes and said, "Zip, sometimes it is good to just stop and enjoy the moment. That is called being mindful. It means paying attention to what is happening right now."

Zip looked puzzled. "What do you mean?"

Tibby patted the bench next to her. "Come and sit with me for a minute."

Curious, Zip hopped up onto the bench. Tibby said, "Close your eyes, take a deep breath, and listen to the different sounds around us."

Zip closed his eyes, took a deep breath, and listened.
He heard the birds singing, the leaves rustling,
and even a distant dog barking.

"Wow, Tibby, I can hear so many things!
But why did I not hear them before?"

"Because you were too busy with so many other things, silly!"
Tibby said with a laugh.

"So, Zip, mindfulness is about paying attention to what is
happening right now. When we are mindful, we notice
the little things we usually miss around us.
It helps us feel calm and happy."

Zip opened his eyes and looked around with new wonder. "I get it, Tibby. Sitting here momentarily and listening to the different sounds makes me feel good inside."

What Is Mindfulness?

Mindfulness means paying attention to the present moment. You are not thinking about yesterday or last week. You are also not thinking about tonight or tomorrow. You are just noticing what is happening right now.

When you are mindful, you focus on what you can see, hear, feel, smell, and taste right now. If you think about it...

Mindfulness is like a superpower for your mind!

Here is why mindfulness is good for kids:

- **It helps you feel calm.** When you are mindful, you take deep breaths and pay attention to your surroundings. This can help you feel more relaxed and less stressed.

- **It helps you improve your focus.** Mindfulness helps you concentrate better. Focusing on your homework, a game, or a story is easier when you pay attention to what is happening right now.

- **It boosts your happiness.** Mindfulness is like happiness juice. Mindfulness can make you feel happier by noticing the good things around you. You learn to appreciate the little things, like a sunny day or a yummy snack.

- **It improves your brain activity and creativity!** Since mindfulness calms you and helps you focus better, your brain works better. This makes it easier to think of new ideas, solve problems, and be creative.

- **It helps you deal with your emotions better.** Mindfulness helps you understand and manage your feelings. Handling big emotions like anger, worry, sadness, or excitement is easier when you know how you feel.

- **It makes you kinder.** Being mindful makes you more aware of how others feel. This can help you be kinder and more understanding towards your friends and family.

Fun Activity #5: Mindful Breathing

This activity will help you feel calm and focused by paying attention to your breath. Let's get started!

1. **Find a comfortable spot.** This could be your favorite chair, your bed, a pillow on the floor, or even outside in a peaceful spot.
2. **Sit comfortably.** You can sit with your legs crossed or your feet flat on the ground. Rest your hands on your lap or knees.
3. **Gently close your eyes.** If you prefer, keep them slightly open and look at a spot on the ground.
4. **Take a deep breath** through your nose. Try to fill your belly with air like a balloon. Then, slowly breathe out through your mouth. Do this a few times.
5. **Focus on your breathing.** Breathe normally and focus on your breath. Notice how the air feels as it goes in and out of your nose. Pay attention to how your chest and belly move with each breath.
6. To help you stay focused, you can **count your breaths**. Count or say "one" as you breathe in and "two" as you breathe out. Keep counting up to ten, and then start again at one.
7. If you start thinking about other things, that is okay! Just notice that you had a thought (oops! I forgot to count), and slowly bring your focus back to your breathing.
8. **Do breath counting for 3-5 minutes.** Every time you lose count or get distracted, just start again. The important thing is to keep bringing your focus back to your breath.
9. After 3-5 minutes, slowly open your eyes and take one last deep breath in and out.

So, how do you feel now compared to when you started? Was breath counting to ten without getting distracted hard? If so, that is okay. You just need more practice.

Do this exercise whenever you feel worried, stressed or overwhelmed. For best results, do your best to breath count until you reach 10, okay?

Fun Activity #6: Mindful Listening

This mindful activity will help you focus and appreciate the sounds around you.

1. **Find a comfortable spot.** This could be your favorite chair, your bed, a pillow on the floor, or even outside in a peaceful spot.
2. **Sit comfortably.** You can sit with your legs crossed or with your feet flat on the ground. Rest your hands on your lap or knees.
3. **Gently close your eyes.** If you prefer, keep them slightly open and look at a spot on the ground.
4. **Take deep breaths.** Take a deep breath through your nose and slowly breathe out through your mouth. Do this a few times to help you relax and get ready to listen.

Start listening. Try to be very still and start to listen to the sounds around you. Try to pick out as many different sounds as you can. Here are some examples of what you might hear:

- birds chirping
- cars driving by
- people talking
- dogs barking
- wind blowing
- someone doing something downstairs
- kids riding bikes

5. **Focus on each sound** for a little while. Notice if the sound is loud or soft. Notice if it is moving closer or farther away. Also, pay attention to how each sound makes you feel. For example, hearing kids riding their bikes might make you happy because you think of doing the same after this exercise.
6. **Sound counting time.** To help you stay focused, count the different sounds you hear. Try to count up to five different sounds. If you hear more, that is great!

7. If you start thinking about other things, that is okay! Just notice that you had a thought (Oops! What was that sound again?), and slowly bring your focus back to listening.
8. **Do sound counting for just 3-5 minutes.** If you get distracted, just start again. The important thing is to keep bringing your focus back to the sounds around you.
9. After 3-5 minutes, slowly open your eyes and take one last deep breath in and out.

How do you feel now compared to when you started? How many sounds did you hear? Did any of them make you feel happy, sad, surprised, or even scared?

Fun Activity #7: Mindful Eating

What is your favorite snack?
___

What is your favorite fruit?
___

What is your favorite vegetable?
___

What is your favorite dinner?
___

This activity is really fun because it will help you enjoy your food even more!

1. **Grab a small piece of food** like a piece of fruit, a raisin, a cracker, or a piece of chocolate.
2. Next, **find a quiet place where you can sit comfortably** with your piece of food. This could be at the kitchen table, couch, or even outside.
3. Before you eat, take a moment to really **look at your food**. Notice its color, shape, and texture. Is it shiny or dull? Smooth or bumpy?
4. Hold the piece of food up to your nose, take a deep breath in, and **smell your food**. How does it smell? Is it sweet, salty, or something else?
5. Next, **gently touch your piece of food**. Notice how it feels in your hand. Is it soft, hard, smooth, or rough?
6. This might seem weird, but hold the piece of food close to your ear. **Does your food make any sound?** Oh yes, sometimes food makes little noises when you squeeze it or move it around a bit.

7. Finally, **take a small bite of your food,** but DO NOT chew it. Notice how it feels in your mouth. What is the texture like? Is it cool or warm? Soft or hard?
8. **Chew very slowly.** Pay attention to the taste and how the taste changes in your mouth as you chew. Notice the different flavors. Is it sweet, sour, salty, or bitter?
9. **Swallow and pause.** Swallow your food, pause for a moment, and notice how your mouth feels. Is there any aftertaste? How does your stomach feel?

Try this exercise with different types of food, and you will be amazed by what you discover. For example, the next time you chew your favorite gum, set a timer and see how long it turns from sweet (or sour) to bland. (I bet it takes longer than you think!)

Of course, during meals, you might not have time to "study" every item on your plate, so pick one food item and eat it very slowly and mindfully.

This activity is cool because you get to TASTE what you eat by eating mindfully. Also, when you make mindful eating a habit, you will enjoy your food more and appreciate who cooked or prepared it better.

Also, mindful eating helps you feel more satisfied with your meals, which may prevent overeating and tummy aches!

Fun Activity #8: Mindfulness Jar

Here is a fun and creative activity called the "Mindful Jar." This activity will help you understand how difficult feelings can settle down, given a little time.

What you will need:
- a clear jar or plastic bottle with a lid
- water
- glitter or glitter glue
- food coloring (optional)
- glue or tape (to seal the lid)

Ask your parents or another adult if you need help gathering your supplies or creating the jar.

1. **Find a comfortable spot** to sit and work on your Mindful Jar.
2. Fill the clear jar or plastic bottle about three-quarters full with water.
3. **Add glitter.** Add a spoonful of glitter to the water. If you use glitter glue, squeeze a small amount into the jar. The glitter represents your thoughts and feelings.

Add food coloring (optional). Add a drop or two of food coloring (any color you like!) to make your jar more colorful. Stir gently to mix everything together.

4. **Close the lid tightly.** You can use glue or tape to seal it so it doesn't accidentally open and spill.
5. **Shake the jar** and watch how the glitter swirls around. This is like when you are upset, worried, or excited—your thoughts and feelings are all mixed up.
6. **Watch the glitter settle.** Put the jar down on a flat surface and watch the glitter slowly settle to the bottom. As you watch, take slow, deep breaths. Notice how you start to feel calmer as the glitter gently glides down. This is like when you take a moment to calm down—your thoughts and feelings settle, too.

Use your Mindfulness Jar whenever you feel upset, worried, or just need a moment to calm down. Shake your Mindful Jar and watch the glitter settle. Take deep breaths and focus on the glitter until it settles completely. Do this as often as you like whenever you feel angry, upset, or anxious.

Cool idea alert: Make different colored jars! Do you remember the Today I feel exercise on page 10? Create matching Mindfulness Jars for each emotion.

Each time you feel a happy emotion, like joy or excitement, add more color or glitter to its matching Mindfulness Jar.

When you feel a not-so-great emotion, shake its corresponding Mindfulness Jar and let the gliding glitter calm you down.

Fun Activity #9: Mindful Coloring

Hi Kids! Have you ever heard of **mandala coloring**? It is a fun and relaxing activity that involves coloring in mandala designs. A mandala is a circular design usually made up of repeating patterns, shapes, and symbols. The word "mandala" comes from an ancient language called Sanskrit (pronounced Sans-kreet), meaning "circle." Cool, huh?

Mandala coloring is great for mindfulness because the repeating patterns and shapes are soothing and help calm your mind. Coloring within the design lines also helps improve concentration and attention to detail, which improves your focus.

1.) Following are two mandala designs. Pick one or do them both; it is all up to you! Use crayons, markers, colored pencils, or other coloring tools. In fact, choose a variety of colors to make your mandala bright and beautiful.

2.) Remember to be mindful. Focus on each section of the mandala as you color. There is no time limit, so just relax, be free, and use whatever color you like.

3.) Every now and then, stop coloring for a moment and look at your picture. Notice how the colors and patterns come together and make you feel.

4.) Put down your coloring tools when you are done or just want to stop. Take a moment to look at your work and appreciate your effort!

Acceptance and Letting Go

Tibby and Zip are at home, cozy and warm, building a BIG tower with colorful blocks. Suddenly, Zip accidentally knocked over the tower, and all the blocks came tumbling down. Zip felt a rush of frustration and disappointment.

"Oh no! I worked so hard on that tower!" Zip exclaimed, his face scrunching up in anger and frustration.

Tibby noticed Zip's upset face and sat down beside him. "It's okay, Zip," she said gently. "Sometimes things don't go how we want them to, and it's important to accept how we feel."

Zip looked at Tibby, still feeling a bit sad. "But I don't like feeling this way! I wanted our tower to be super high and perfect."

Tibby nodded understandingly. "I know, Zip. But accepting how you feel about what happened will help you feel better faster."

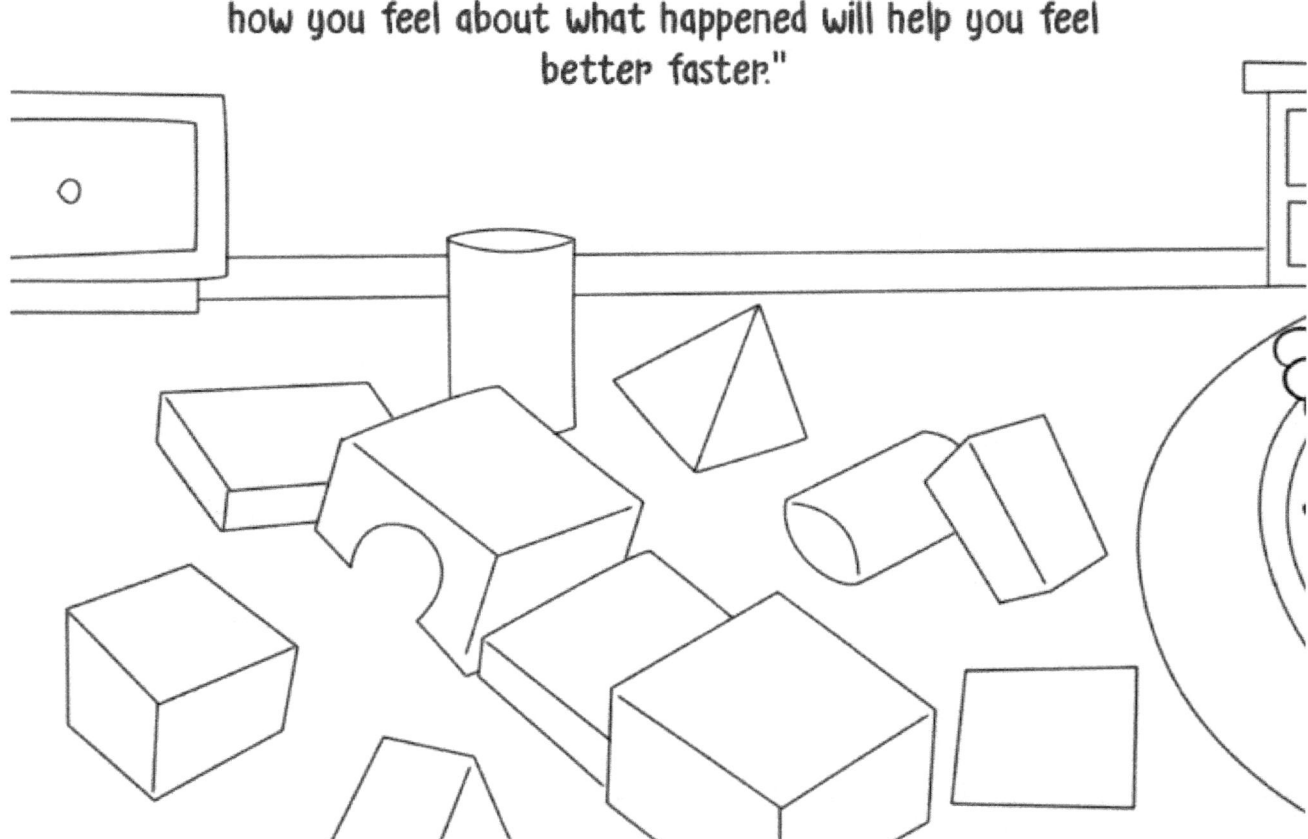

"How, Tibby?" Zip asked, looking very puzzled.

"Well, if you stay frustrated and mad, you probably won't
be in the mood to build another tower, right?
But, if you accept what happened and let your anger go...
then we can start building another tower or
play something else in the very next minute!"

Zip looked up at Tibby, beamed a bright, sunny smile, and said, "Hmmm… you're right, big kitty sis! If I accept what happened sooner, I'll feel better sooner!"

"So, do you feel better now, Zip?"

"Yep, let's take out our coloring books!"

What Is Acceptance?

Acceptance means letting yourself feel your emotions without trying to change them or make them disappear. It's like saying, "All's good. It's okay to feel this way." When you accept your feelings—no matter how unpleasant or difficult they are—you'll feel more at peace with what happened and can feel better sooner!

What is "Letting Go"?

Accepting your feelings doesn't mean keeping them. Remember what happened to Zip's tower? He accepted that it came crashing down and that he felt really frustrated and mad. But after accepting what happened, he let go of all his negative feelings and could move on and play happily again!

Why It's Sometimes Important to NOT Act on Our Feelings

Another reason why it's super important to accept and let go of unhelpful thoughts and feelings is so that you can stay calm and not get overwhelmed. You see, sometimes, our feelings can make us want to do things that aren't helpful or kind.

For example, what if Zip didn't accept what happened and didn't let go of his anger? He might kick or throw his blocks in frustration and make a bigger mess. Worse, he might hit Tibby!

But by accepting what happened and letting go of his frustration and anger instead of acting based on them, Zip could calm himself, feel better, and make a much better choice. (To take out and play with their coloring books!)

Remember, it's okay to feel all kinds of emotions. Accepting them is the first step to letting them go and feeling more at peace. Let's keep exploring and learning more about acceptance and letting go in the next pages!

Fun Activity #10: Balloon Release

Hi kids! This activity will help you practice accepting your feelings and letting go of the ones that bother you. Let's get started!

What you will need:
- a quiet place to sit
- pieces of paper or a notebook
- crayons, markers, or colored pencils
- scissors (with adult supervision)

Ask your parents or another adult if you need help gathering your supplies or doing this exercise.

1. **Find a comfortable spot.** This could be at the kitchen table, on the floor, or in your room.

2. Get a big sheet of paper or open your notebook, and then, using your crayons, markers, or colored pencils, **draw a BIG balloon**. For example, you can draw a bright red balloon on your paper if you're mad about something.

   You can also cut out the big balloon on the right and use that.

   Using a pen or one of your colored pencils, **write down a feeling that's been bothering you inside the balloon**. For example, you can write, "I feel angry because my friend didn't want to play with me."

3. Next, **get your scissors and carefully cut out the balloon shape from your paper**. Remember, ask an adult for help if you need it.

4. **Practice acceptance**: Hold your paper balloon in your hands. Close your eyes and take a deep breath in. Imagine your breath filling the balloon with all the feelings you wrote or drew.

   Tell yourself it's okay to feel what you're feeling. Everyone has these feelings sometimes. Take a moment to accept your feelings without trying to change them.

5. **Practice letting go**: As you breathe out, let go of the cut-up balloon in your hand. (If you want, you can crumple the balloon cutout before you let it go.) Imagine this as a symbol of letting go of the feelings that are bothering you.

Cool idea, alert! You can ask an adult to get you a real balloon if you want. Hold the string tight and take a deep breath in. As you do, imagine transferring any unhelpful or unpleasant feeling inside your balloon. Breathe out and open your hand, letting go of the string. Watch the balloon float away until it's out of sight.

Whew! How do you feel after doing this exercise? Do you feel a little lighter or calmer? It's okay if the feeling doesn't go away completely. The important thing is that you practice letting it go. You should feel really good and proud of yourself for that.

Fun Activity #11: The Worry Box

Are you worried about something? Perhaps you're worried about an upcoming test or project at school or feeling nervous about making new friends. Whenever you're worried, do this activity. It will help you manage your worries by putting them in a special box.

What you will need:
- a small box like a tissue box or shoe box
- paper (you can use colored paper if you like)
- crayons, markers, or colored pencils
- scissors (ask an adult for help)
- tape or glue
- stickers or other decorations (optional)

Ask your parents or another adult if you need help gathering your supplies or doing this exercise.

1. **Find a comfortable spot.** This could be at the kitchen table, on the floor, or in your room.

2. **Take your box and decorate it** however you like. Use crayons, markers, stickers, and other decorations to make it your own special Worry Box. You can write your name on it or draw pictures that make you feel happy.

3. **Make worry slips**: Next, get a piece of paper and cut it into small pieces or squares. These will be your worry slips, where you will write down your worries. (You can ask an adult for help when using scissors.)

4. **Write down your worries**: Whenever you're worried about something, take a worry slip and write or draw what you're worried about.

Example: **Worry slip #1: I'm worried about my math test**
Worry slip #1:
Worry slip #2:
Worry slip #3:
Worry slip #4:
Worry slip #5:
Worry slip #6:
Worry slip #7:
Worry slip #8:

5. After you write down your worry, **fold your worry slip** and hold it in your hands for a moment. Take a deep breath in and out, then place it in your Worry Box.

6. Once your worry is in the box, imagine it leaving your mind and staying in the box. This will help you feel lighter and less worried.

If you want, you can set a special time each day to look at your worries. With the help of a parent or an adult, you can decide if you still need to worry about them or if it's time to let the worry go.

At the end of the week or when you feel ready, you can empty your Worry Box. Look at the worries and see if they still bother you. If not, throw them away as a way of letting them go.

Fun Activity #12: I'm a Good Kid

Ready to feel good? Sometimes, when you have a feeling that's bothering you inside, you can feel really down and gloomy. So, in this activity, you will write "positive affirmations."

These are kind and encouraging words that you say to yourself. They help you feel good about who you are and what you can do, boosting your self-confidence. Positive affirmations also help you focus on good thoughts, helping you develop a positive mindset.

What you will need:
- crayons, markers, or colored pencils
- a notebook or journal
- a mirror (optional)

1. **Find a comfortable spot.** This could be at the kitchen table, on the floor, or in your room.

2. Get your notebook and crayons, markers, or colored pencils out. Next, **write down at least five** really good things (positive affirmations) about yourself. For example, you can write any of the following:

    ☐ I am a good friend.
    ☐ I am kind to others.
    ☐ I am great at drawing.
    ☐ I help my family.
    ☐ I am brave.
    ☐ I am good at sports.
    ☐ I am smart.
    ☐ I am funny and make people laugh.
    ☐ I am creative.

- ☐ I am a good listener.
- ☐ I am helpful in the classroom.
- ☐ I am good at solving puzzles.
- ☐ I am caring towards animals.
- ☐ I am patient.
- ☐ I am a good reader.
- ☐ I have a great imagination.
- ☐ I am honest.
- ☐ I am good at building things.
- ☐ I am respectful to others.
- ☐ I am good at sharing.
- ☐ I am good at singing.
- ☐ I am good at dancing.
- ☐ I am good at baking/cooking.
- ☐ I am thoughtful.
- ☐ I am good at remembering things.

My positive affirmations are:

Feel free to decorate your affirmations as much as you like. Use crayons, markers, or colored pencils, draw pictures, or even use stickers that match your affirmations or add fun designs.

3. **Read your affirmations out loud!** After decorating your positive affirmations, hold your paper and read each affirmation aloud. If you have a mirror, stand in front of it and look at yourself while you say each affirmation. Say them with confidence and really BELIEVE in the words you're saying.

   Cool idea, alert! Make it a habit to read your affirmations every day. You can do it in the morning when you wake up, before bed, or anytime you need a little confidence boost.

4. **Add more affirmations**: Add them to your notebook as you think of more positive things about yourself. The more affirmations you have, the better you'll feel!

FREE GUIDE: Mental Health Boosters for Kids

FREE DOWNLOAD ALERT!

Fun and Engaging Activities to Manage Your Children's Emotional Well-Being

https://barretthuang.com/mental-health-boosters/

Or scan the code below:

Learning About Your Thoughts

One bright afternoon in Kittyville,
Tibby and Zip are playing in their favorite park.
The sun is shining, and the birds are singing.
Tibby is teaching Zip how to climb the big oak tree.
Zip is excited but also a little nervous.

"What is it, Zip?" Tibby asked gently.

"I don't know if I can do it, Tibby," Zip said, looking up at the tall tree.

"Why are you having doubts, Zip?"

"I have a thought I might fall," Zip admitted, his whiskers twitching with worry.

Tibby smiled and gave Zip a comforting nuzzle. "Thoughts can be tricky, Zip. But just because you have a thought doesn't mean it's true. Learning about our thoughts and understanding how they work is important."

Zip tilted his head curiously. "What do you mean, Tibby?"

"Well," Tibby began, "you thought you might fall if you climbed the tree, right? But that's not a sure thing, Zip. If you carefully climb the tree, you might not fall. Instead, you might have lots and lots of fun seeing the view from up there."

"Oh, so what do I do with the thought I just had?" asked Zip.

"That's a great question, Zip," Tibby replied. "When you have a thought like that, you can challenge it. Ask yourself if it's really true or if it's just something you're worried about. Let's think about all the times you've climbed smaller trees without falling."

Zip thought for a moment and nodded. "You're right, Tibby. I didn't fall those times."

"Exactly," Tibby said encouragingly. "You can also focus on what you can do to stay safe. Use your claws to grip the bark, take it slow, and pay attention to where you're stepping."

Zip took a deep breath, feeling a bit more confident. "Okay, Tibby, I'm ready to try it."

With Tibby's guidance, Zip carefully climbed the big oak tree. He took it one step at a time, remembering Tibby's advice. As he climbed higher, he felt his confidence growing. Soon, he was halfway up the tree.

"You're doing great, Zip!" Tibby cheered from below. "Look how far you've come!"

Zip looked down and realized he was doing it. He was actually climbing the big oak tree. "I am, Tibby! I'm really doing it!"

Finally, Zip reached a sturdy branch near the top and looked out over the park. The view was amazing. He could see the entire park, the sparkling pond, and the rooftops of Kittyville.

Tibby climbed up to join Zip, and together they enjoyed the view. "I'm proud of you, Zip," Tibby said. "You faced your fear and proved to yourself that you can do it."

"Wow, Tibby, this is incredible," Zip exclaimed. "I'm so glad I didn't let my worries stop me!"

What Are Thoughts?

Thoughts are the words and pictures that pop into your head. They are like a little voice inside your mind that talks to you. You can have all kinds of thoughts. You can have positive thoughts, and you can have negative thoughts.

Here are examples of positive thoughts:
- This is hard, but I can do this!
- I am proud of myself.
- It's okay if I make a mistake. I'll learn from it.

Here are examples of negative thoughts:
- This is going to be too hard for me.
- What if I make a mistake? The other kids will laugh at me.
- For sure, I'm going to fail!

Positive thoughts are great; they make you feel good about yourself and encourage you to try new things. They help you believe in yourself and keep going, even when things are tough.

Negative thoughts, on the other hand, can make you feel bad and stop you from trying your best. They can scare or worry you and keep you from doing things you enjoy or learning new skills.

So, negative thoughts are not very helpful, but do you know what's amazing? You are the boss of your thoughts!

That's right. Whenever you have a negative thought, you can let it go or try to change it into a positive one.

Understanding Thoughts vs. Reality

Thoughts happen in your mind. Sometimes they are true, and sometimes they are not. For example, you might remember a fun time with your friends that already happened. So, that's a TRUE thought or fact.

Sometimes, thoughts are not true but are more like... worries. For example, you might think that everyone will laugh IF you make a mistake while reading out loud in class.

Reality is what is actually happening around you. It's the real world that you can see, touch, hear, and experience. Reality is the truth, no matter what your thoughts say. It's important to know the difference between thoughts and reality because sometimes, our thoughts can trick us!

For example, suppose you're at the school playground and have the thought, "Everyone is looking at me." This thought might make you shy, so you get up and walk back inside your school.

In reality, not everyone is looking at you, and when you stand up and walk away, a classmate is just about to go over to you and say, "Hi." Oh, no! You missed making a new friend!

So, you see, it's important to understand that some thoughts are just not real. And whenever you have an unhelpful thought, it's important just to let them come and go.

Fun Activity #13: Thought Bubbles

This fun activity will help you see your thoughts and how they make you feel. When you find yourself thinking unhelpful thoughts, it will also help you focus on things that would lift your spirits.

What you will need:
- crayons, markers, or colored pencils
- pieces of paper, or a notebook or journal
- stickers (optional)

1. Get your crayons, markers, or colored pencils out. If you want to use stickers, you can do that too.

2. Close your eyes for a moment and think about some thoughts you've had recently. They could be thoughts about school, home, or playing with friends.

3. Open your eyes and write or draw one thought inside one of the Thought Bubbles below. Here are some examples to get you started:

    - Thought: *I think I did great on my test!*
    - Thought: *What if I don't have anyone to play with at recess?*
    - Thought: *I'm excited about my birthday party!*
    - Thought: *I'm worried about my homework.*
    - Thought: *I think Mom and Dad are mad at me.*

    There are five Thought Bubbles below, but if you have more thoughts or want more space, you can get a piece of paper and draw extra thought bubbles.

4. After writing a thought in one of the Thought Bubbles, color it or put stickers to help you express your feelings about that thought. For example, you might use bright colors like yellow or green for happy thoughts and darker colors like blue or gray for sad or unpleasant thoughts.

IMPORTANT: You can have any thought you want. All your thoughts are okay.

5. Now, look back at your Thought Bubbles masterpiece! You did a great job trying to express your thoughts.

6. Now, pick out a happy or helpful thought from your Thought Bubbles and think about how it makes you feel. Here's an example:
   Helpful Thought: I think I did great on my test!
   What it makes me feel: I feel good and proud of myself!

7. Next, can you pick an **Unhelpful Thought** above? These thoughts make you feel worried, sad, or scared. Sometimes, unhelpful thoughts stop you from doing what you want to do. Here's an example:

   Unhelpful Thought: What if I don't have anyone to play with at recess?
   Effect: This thought might stop you from going over and saying "Hi" to your classmates at school and inviting them to play. This means that this thought made you shy. And since you didn't play with anyone, this thought might have made you lonely.

   Important: If you find it hard to identify an unhelpful thought, ask the help of one of your **Safe People**.

8. **Do a switcheroo!** After identifying an unhelpful thought, see if you can replace it with a helpful one. Here's an example**:**

   Unhelpful Thought: What if I don't have anyone to play with at recess?
   Helpful Thought: I can ask someone new in my class to play with me.

   Now, close your eyes and imagine if you followed Helpful Thought instead of Unhelpful Thought. Isn't playing with someone so much better?

9. **Keep practicing!** Make new Thought Bubbles whenever you need to. The more you practice, the better you'll get at spotting helpful thoughts and feeling good about them. You'll also get better at noticing unhelpful thoughts and changing them.

Fun Activity #14: Thought Train

It's great if you can easily turn Unhelpful Thoughts into Helpful Thoughts. But, sometimes, sad or unhelpful thoughts stay with you and can affect your feelings and behaviors. Remember our example from the previous exercise?

Unhelpful Thought: What if I don't have anyone to play with at recess?
Effect on Your Feelings: You might feel *worried* or *sad*. You might even feel *embarrassed* just at the thought that you'll be seen all alone with no one to play with at school.
Effect on Your Behavior: You might want to skip school.

Maybe it's okay to skip school once if your parents allow it, but what about tomorrow? You can't keep on skipping school, right?

So, here's a fun exercise for you to do whenever you get an Unhelpful Thought. Think of it as a train that arrives in your mind... and choo-choos away. Let's try it!

1. Close your eyes and think of an unhelpful thought you've been thinking about lately. For example: No one likes me.

2. Imagine that thought like a train arriving at a train station.

3. Sometimes, when the train (thought) arrives, it just zooms past the train station (your mind). Other times, it stops for a while (in your mind), and you may start to feel not-so-happy emotions when this happens. For example, you might start to feel sad or angry.

   It's okay to feel these feelings. Just do some <u>Mindful Breathing</u> like you did on page 58. Imagine helping the train pass by with each strong exhale you make!

4. Watch the train leave your mind because that's exactly what thoughts do—they come and go.

You are NOT Your Thoughts

Now, kids, it's VERY important to know that even though you can think so many things in your mind, you're NOT your thoughts.

For example, let's say you're thinking you're a fireman. That's a great thought. It means you're brave and want to help others. But you're not a fireman *yet*, so it's important to remember that some thoughts are just ideas and not who you are right now.

Sadly, not all the thoughts we have about ourselves are good. For example, you may have the thought, "I'm invisible. No one listens to me." Now, that's just not true, is it? NO ONE is invisible!

So, you see, even though you think you're invisible, in reality, you're not, and it's important just to let this thought pass by. Just let it come and go, and don't believe it.

Fun Activity #15: Clouds in the Sky

This activity will help you learn how to watch your thoughts come and go like clouds in the sky.

1. **Find a comfortable spot.** This could be your favorite chair, a cushion on the floor, or even outside in a peaceful spot.

2. **Sit down comfortably.** You can sit with your legs crossed or with your feet flat on the ground. Rest your hands on your lap or knees. **Gently close your eyes.**

3. **Imagine a big, clear blue sky in your mind.** This sky is wide and open, with lots of space for clouds to float by.

4. **When a thought comes into your mind, picture it as a cloud.** Some thoughts might be happy, some might be sad, and some might be silly. Whatever the thought is, just watch it float by in your mind's sky.

Important: If you start to follow a thought (or cloud), slowly bring your focus back to watching it pass by. Remember, you are just watching the clouds come and go, not chasing them.

5. Take slow, deep breaths through your nose and out through your mouth. As you breathe, keep watching your thoughts float by like clouds.

6. When you feel ready, slowly open your eyes. Take one last deep breath in and out, and notice how calm and peaceful you feel.

Fun Activity #16: Mountain Meditation

Sometimes, no matter how we want unhelpful thoughts and feelings to pass by like clouds really, really fast... some tend to stay longer than we want. But, you know what? That's okay because YOU are a mighty mountain!

1. **Find a comfortable spot.** This could be your favorite chair, a cushion on the floor, or even outside in a peaceful spot.

2. **Sit down comfortably.** You can sit with your legs crossed or with your feet flat on the ground. Rest your hands on your lap or knees. **Gently close your eyes.**

3. **Imagine a big, strong mountain in your mind.** Think about how tall and steady it is. No matter the weather—sunny, rainy, or windy—the mountain stays strong and still.

    Now, imagine that YOU are the mountain. Feel yourself sitting tall and steady. Your body is strong like the mountain, and you are not moved by the weather (your thoughts and feelings).

4. **Take slow, deep breaths** through your nose and out through your mouth. As you breathe, feel your body become even more steady and strong.

5. While you're sitting like a mountain, you might notice different thoughts and feelings. For example, you might suddenly think, "I forgot my books!" or you might suddenly feel hungry. That's okay; just imagine watching these thoughts and feelings come and go like clouds passing a mountain.

    Remember, YOU are the mountain. Thoughts and feelings are just like the weather—they come and go, but you stay steady and strong.

6. When a thought or feeling comes, just notice it and then let it pass. You don't need to follow it or get caught up in it. You are the mountain, and you stay strong no matter what!
7. When you feel ready, slowly open your eyes. Take one last deep breath in and out, and notice how calm and strong you feel.

Fun Activity #17: Thought Untangling Cards

Hey kids, here's something that makes unhelpful thoughts and difficult feelings pass by quickly: Do something fun!

For this activity, you're going to use Thought Untangling Cards. Pick one whenever you're bothered with unhelpful thoughts so you can see them in a fun or less serious way. By changing how you look at your thoughts, you can feel calmer and more in control. Remember, thoughts are just things your mind says—they aren't always true.

Now, let's explore these six techniques together!

1. **Leaves on a Stream.** Imagine your thoughts as leaves floating down a stream. Watch each leaf (thought) float by and disappear downstream. This helps you let go of your thoughts.

    For example, picture the thought "I'm worried about my test" as a leaf on a stream. Watch it float away and disappear, leaving you feeling a lot calmer.

2. **Silly Voices.** Imagine your thoughts being said in a funny or silly voice, like a cartoon character or a robot. This can make the thought seem less serious and help you feel better.

    For example, if you're thinking, "I can't do this," imagine it being said in a squeaky mouse or robot voice. It might make you giggle and feel less worried!

3. **Soap Bubbles.** Pretend that your unwanted thoughts or feelings are floating in soap bubbles. Watch them float away or... pop them! This helps you see that thoughts come and go, like bubbles, and that YOU can make them go away if you want to.
    For example, picture the thought, "I'm scared of the dark," in a soap bubble. Watch the bubble float up, or pop it! Poof! The thought is gone.

Cool idea alert: If you have a soap bubble gun or machine, don't just imagine soap bubbles; make them!

4. **Name That Story.** Give your thoughts a name, like a storybook title. This helps you see that it's just a story your mind tells. It's not something that's necessarily true.

   For example, if you keep thinking, "I'm not good at math," call it "The Math Worry Story." When the thought comes up, you can say, "Oh, there's the Math Worry Story again! Hahaha."

5. **Sing Your Thoughts.** Sing your thoughts to the tune of a favorite song. This makes the thought seem less serious and can make you feel more relaxed and happy.

   For example, if you're thinking, "I'll never finish my homework," try singing it to the tune of "Twinkle, Twinkle, Little Star." That will surely make the thought feel less scary!

6. **Friendly Monster.** Draw a picture of a friendly monster who says your tricky thoughts. This way, you can kindly talk back to the monster and understand that your thoughts aren't that scary.

   For example, draw a cute monster and name it something fun, like "Fuzzy." When you think, "I'm afraid of trying new things," imagine Fuzzy saying it. Then, you can say, "Thanks for sharing, Fuzzy, but I will try anyway!"

THOUGHT UNTANGLING CARDS

Knowing What Matters

Tibby and Zip are playing in their backyard. They set up a fun obstacle course and take turns racing through it with their toys. Tibby is timing Zip as he tries to beat his best score.

On his last run, Zip tripped over a toy car and fell. He quickly picked himself up and finished the course but looked a little worried.

"How did I do, Tibby?" Zip asked, catching his breath.

Tibby checked the timer. "You were super-fast, Zip, but you skipped one of the jumps."

Zip hesitated, then shrugged.
"Uh, yeah, I skipped it on purpose. It was faster that way,"
he said, trying to sound confident.

Tibby frowned a little but then smiled gently.
"Zip, I know you want to have the best time,
but skipping a jump to finish faster isn't fair.
It's important to be HONEST about what happened."

"I just really wanted to win."

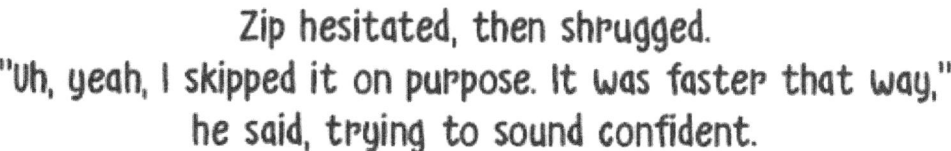

"HONESTY is an important value, Zip, because it helps people trust us and know we're telling the truth. Cheating might make you feel good for a teeny tiny moment, but being honest makes you feel good inside for a long time."

Zip nodded slowly. "You're right, Tibby. I should always tell the truth."

"Exactly," Tibby said, hugging him. "Honesty makes us feel good because we know we're doing the right thing."

What Are Values?

Values are the things that are really important to us. They guide how we behave and make decisions. Values help us know what's right and wrong and show us how to live a good and happy life.

Here are some examples of values that you may have:

- **Kindness** is being nice and being willing to help others. For example, helping a friend with their homework when they are struggling.
- **Honesty** is telling the truth and being trustworthy. For example, admitting to your parents when you accidentally break something.
- **Bravery** is being courageous and standing up for what's right. For example, telling a teacher if someone in class is being bullied.
- **Creativity** is using your imagination and creating new things. For example, drawing a picture of a magical world you've imagined.
- **Respect** is treating others with care and understanding. For example, listening to your friend's ideas without interrupting them.
- **Responsibility** is taking care of your duties and being dependable. For example, feeding your pet every day without being reminded.

- **Friendship** is being a good friend and supporting others. For example, cheering up a friend who is feeling sad.

Values help you make good choices and decide how to act in different situations. And when you behave according to your values, you'll feel proud and happy because you know you're doing the right thing.

On the other hand, if you don't act according to your values, you'll feel sad and maybe a little bit bad inside. For example, if honesty is important to you, but you tell a lie, you might feel guilty or ashamed. These feelings can make you unhappy and uncomfortable.

Also, if you don't follow your values, people might find it hard to trust you. Trust is important in friendships and family relationships. You want people to like and trust you, don't you?

Lastly, not behaving according to your values means you might say or do something you'll regret later. For example, suppose you value friendship, but when a friend asks if they can come over because they're sad, you lie and say your parents aren't allowing visitors today. Soon enough, you feel really bad for not being there for your friend. Acting against your values can lead to sadness or regret.

What's regret? It's like wishing you could go back and change something you did. For example, imagine choosing between a healthy snack, like a piece of fruit, and a donut. You chose the donut, but then it gave you a tummy ache. Now, you wish you had eaten the fruit instead. That's what regret feels like.

So, it's super important to know your values and to behave according to them. Now, let's go on a discovery mission and find out your values!

Fun Activity #18: Values BINGO

Here's a fun game called Values Bingo. This game will help you learn about and practice different values over a week. Let's get started!

1. **Understanding the values on the bingo card.** Before you start, understand what each value on the Values Bingo card means. Here are the values on the card and what they represent:

   - **Honesty**: Telling the truth. For example, admitting to your parents when you accidentally break something.
   - **Respect**: Treating others with care. For example, listening to your friend's ideas without interrupting them.
   - **Gratitude**: Being thankful. For example, saying "Thank You" when someone gives you a gift.
   - **Responsibility**: Taking care of your duties. For example, feeding your pet every day without being reminded.
   - **Cleanliness**: Keeping yourself and your surroundings clean. For example, washing your hands before eating.
   - **Patience**: Waiting calmly for something. For example, waiting your turn to speak in class.
   - **Empathy**: Understanding and caring about how others feel and doing your best to share their feelings. For example, if you see a friend who is upset, you might want to imagine feeling that way, too, if you were in their shoes.
   - **Politeness**: Being courteous and using good manners. Courteous means being kind and polite to others. It's like saying "please" and "thank you."
   - **Bravery**: Being courageous and standing up for what's right. It's doing something because it's the right thing to do, even when it's something a little scary. For example, telling a teacher if someone is being bullied.

- **Kindness**: Being nice and helping others. For example, helping a friend with their homework when they are struggling.
- **Creativity**: Using your imagination. For example, drawing a picture of a magical world you've imagined.
- **Friendship**: Being a good friend. For example, cheering up a friend who is feeling sad.

2. **Your goal:** Practice each value on the Values Bingo card over the next week. You can do this at home, school, or anywhere.

3. **Each time you practice a value, mark it off on your Values Bingo card** with a sticker, marker, colored pencil, or anything you like! You can also write a little note about what you did to practice that value.

4. At the end of the week, look at your Values Bingo card and see how many values you've practiced. Think about how practicing these values made you feel and how it might have helped others around you!

MY VALUES BINGO

HONESTY	RESPECT	GRATITUDE
RESPONSIBILITY	CLEANLINESS	PATIENCE
EMPATHY	POLITENESS	BRAVERY
KINDNESS	FRIENDSHIP	CREATIVITY

Fun Activity #19: Likes and Dislikes

Confused about your values? That's okay. This activity will help you discover the values and behaviors you DON'T like, which can help you understand what values are important to you. Does that sound confusing? Don't worry; do the activity and learn what it means!

What you will need:
- crayons, markers, or colored pencils
- pieces of paper, or a notebook or journal

Ask your parents or another adult if you need help with this exercise.

1. **Find a comfortable spot.** This could be your favorite chair, a cushion on the floor, or even outside in a peaceful spot.

2. Take a piece of paper (or open your notebook or journal) and draw a line down the middle, creating two columns. At the top of the left column, write "I Don't Like." At the top of the right column, write "Value I Like."

3. Next, **think about different behaviors and actions that you don't like**. These could be things you've seen at school, home or on TV. For example, if you don't like it when people are mean, write "Being mean" in the left column.

VALUE I DON'T LIKE	VALUE I LIKE
Being mean	

4. Now, **for every behavior or action you don't like, think about the value that is the <u>opposite</u> of it**. Write this value in the right column. For example, if you wrote "Being mean" in the left column, you could write "Kindness" in the right column.

   Here's another example: if you don't like it when people are "telling lies," that means the value important to you is "honesty."

   If you need help, ask your parents or an adult to help you fill out the table below.

VALUE I DON'T LIKE	VALUE I LIKE
Being mean	kindness
Telling lies	honesty

5. Now, for the really fun part: **decorate your page**! Use your crayons, markers, or colored pencils to decorate your page. You can draw pictures next to each value to illustrate what it looks like.

6. After creating your Likes & Dislikes page, think about how you can show or act according to the values you like. For example, if you value *kindness*, you might want to write down, "help Mom/Dad water the plants tomorrow."

VALUE I DON'T LIKE	VALUE I LIKE	WHAT TO DO
Being mean	kindness	Share my toys
Telling lies	honesty	Tell Mom/Dad I forgot to do my homework

Fun Activity #20: It's My Birthday! It's My Birthday!

Here's a fun and imaginative activity called It's My Birthday! This activity will help you think about what's really important to you (values) by imagining what you want people to say about you on your birthday. Let's get started!

What you will need:
- crayons, markers, or colored pencils
- pieces of paper, or a notebook or journal

1. **Find a comfortable spot.** This could be at the kitchen table, in your room, or outside in a peaceful spot.

2. **Close your eyes and imagine it's your birthday.** Think about everyone present at your party, the celebration, and what you wish everyone would say about you.

3. Open your eyes and draw a picture of your special birthday celebration on a piece of paper (or in your notebook or journal). Include the people who are important to you and the activities that make you happy. Make your birthday page as fun, colorful, and amazing as you like! Draw different colored balloons, put a cake sticker, etc.

4. Next, **imagine what the people at your birthday party say about you**. What could they say that would make you feel proud and happy? Write down a few things they might say. Here are some examples:

    - *You are so kind and always help others.*
    - *You are honest and always tell the truth.*
    - *You are creative and come up with great ideas.*

- *You are brave and try new things.*
- *You are a good friend and always listen.*
- *You are responsible and always do your chores.*
- *You are respectful and treat everyone nicely.*
- *You always like to share what you have.*
- *You are funny and make everyone laugh!*
- *You are thoughtful and always think of others.*

5. Look at your list and think about the values these represent. For example, if you want someone to say, "You are funny and make everyone laugh!" then this might mean you value humor.

What I Wish People Would Say About Me On My Birthday	Value Meaning
Example: *You always like to share what you have.*	*Example:* *Generosity*

Doing What Matters

Tibby and Zip are playing with their toys in their backyard. Suddenly, they heard a loud cry from the other side of the fence!

Tibby and Zip peeked over the fence and saw their neighbor, Sammy the squirrel, looking very upset. His kite was stuck high in a tree, and he couldn't get it down.

"Don't worry, Sammy, we'll help you!" Zip said. He then turned to Tibby and said, "One of our values is KINDNESS, so we should definitely help Sammy because that's the kind thing to do, right Tibby?"

"Absolutely, Zip!" Tibby agreed. "And another one of our values is BRAVERY. We might need to be brave enough to climb and get Sammy's kite."

Together, Tibby and Zip carefully climbed the tree. Zip held the branches steady while Tibby reached up and grabbed the kite. They worked as a team and soon had the kite safely back with Sammy.

"Thank you so much, Tibby and Zip!" Sammy said, smiling with relief. "You guys are the best!"

What "Doing What Matters" Mean

Doing what matters means making choices and acting in ways that show your values. It's about behaving in a way that shows to yourself and to everyone what's important to you. You feel proud and happy when you act according to your values because you're true to yourself.

You see, kids, values are not secrets to keep inside. They should be shown—through your actions—for all to see! Let's explore and learn more about acting on values and doing what matters together!

Fun Activity #21: Doing What Matters Schedule

This activity will help you plan your day or week by including actions that show your values. Let's get started!

1. **Find a comfortable spot.** This could be at the kitchen table, in your room, or even outside in a peaceful spot.

2. On the schedule below, **write a value you want to "put in action"** and when you want to do it. If possible, try to practice different kinds of values throughout your day.

Monday	Morning	After	Evening
Example:	*Value*: Kindness *What to do*: Help make breakfast.	*Value*: Politeness *What to do*: Say "Please" when I ask for something.	*Value*: Responsibility *What to do*: Finish my chores and homework on time.
Monday	Morning	After	Evening
Tuesday	Morning	After	Evening

Wednesday	Morning	After	Evening
Thursday	Morning	After	Evening
Friday	Morning	After	Evening
Saturday	Morning	After	Evening
Sunday	Morning	After	Evening

3. **Make your schedule fun!** Use your crayons, markers, or colored pencils to decorate your schedule. You can also draw pictures or paste stickers that show your values and what you did to show them.

4. **Review and do!** Look at your schedule each day and remind yourself of the actions you planned. Try to follow your schedule for the whole week. You can do it!

Fun Activity #22: I'm a SMART Kid

This activity will teach you how to set goals using the S.M.A.R.T. technique. This special technique is something grown-ups use, but I know you're amazing enough to do it, too. So let's get started!

First things first, what does SMART mean, anyway? How will it help you achieve the things you want to do?

SMART stands for:

Specific: This means that your goal should be super clear and specific.
Example: "I want to start and finish reading ONE book."
Measurable: This means you should be able to keep track of your progress.
Example: "I will read one chapter every day so I meet my goal."
Achievable: This means your goal should be something that you can actually reach.
Example: "I will choose a book that is not too long and that I find really interesting."
Relevant: This means that your goal should be important to you.
Example: "I love reading and learning new things, so this goal is important to me."
Time-bound: This means setting a time limit for your goal.
Example: "I will finish reading ONE book in ONE month."

Now that you understand what SMART means let's make one!

1. **Find a comfortable spot.** This could be at the kitchen table, in your room, or even outside in a peaceful spot.

2. **Think about what matters to you (values).** Let your values dictate the goal you want to set.

3. Here we go: Use the SMART technique to set a goal! Write down your goal in the right column.

VALUE: *Example:* *Responsibility*	MY VALUE:	MY VALUE:	MY VALUE:
Specific: *Example: I want to put the value of RESPONSIBILITY in action.*	**S**pecific:	**S**pecific:	**S**pecific:
Measurable: *Example: I will clean my room every Saturday*	**M**easurable:	**M**easurable:	**M**easurable:
Achievable: *Example: I can set aside 30 minutes each Saturday to clean my room.*	**A**chievable:	**A**chievable:	**A**chievable:

Relevant: *Example: Responsibility is important to me because I want to be a kid people can trust or depend on. For example, when they ask me to do something, they believe I will do it. I don't like people doubting me.*	**R**elevant:	**R**elevant:	**R**elevant:
Time-bound: *Example: I will clean my room every Saturday for two months.*	**T**ime-bound:	**T**ime-bound:	**T**ime-bound:

5. Ask your parent or an adult to **print your SMART table** so you can put it up and see it every day, like on your bedroom wall or the fridge. This will remind you to work towards your goal.

    Cool idea, alert! Create your own SMART table using colored paper and decorate it with crayons, markers, colored pencils, stickers, etc.

6. To help you achieve your SMART goal, **create a schedule**! For example, if your goal is to clean your room every Saturday for the next two months, then your SMART schedule should look like this:

SMART Schedule	Did I Clean My Room?
Example: January, 1st Saturday	✓
January, 1st Saturday	
January, 2nd Saturday	
January, 2nd Saturday	
January, 4th Saturday	
February, 1st Saturday	
February, 2nd Saturday	
February, 3rd Saturday	
February, 4th Saturday	

Put a BIG checkmark whenever you do what you set out to do for that day to achieve your ultimate goal. This will help you see your progress and stay motivated!

W.O.O.P. Your Goal!

You set and achieve your goals by thinking about your **W**ish, the **O**utcome (result) you want, the **O**bstacles (challenges) you might face, and your **P**lan to overcome them.

1. **Find a comfortable spot.** This could be at the kitchen table, in your room, or even outside in a peaceful spot.

2. Fill out the **WOOP** table below.

W.O.O.P. Your Goal!			
Wish What is your wish? What do you want to happen? *Example: I want to get better at playing the piano.*	**Wish**	**Wish**	**Wish**
Outcome What will happen if your wish comes true? Imagine what the result would be like. *Example: I can play my favorite song perfectly and feel proud and happy.*	**Outcome**	**Outcome**	**Outcome**

Obstacles What challenges could make it hard for you to achieve your wish? *Examples:* *- If I make mistakes, I might get frustrated and stop practicing.* *- I might not have enough time to practice every day.*	**Obstacles**	**Obstacles**	**Obstacles**
Plan What's your plan to overcome your obstacles? Think about what you can do to keep going even when it's tough. *Example:* *- I will remind myself that making mistakes is okay and part of learning.* *- I will set a specific time to practice for at least 15 minutes each day. I will ask Mom and Dad if I can have "alone time" when I get home from school to have these 15 minutes.*	**Plan**	**Plan**	**Plan**

Fun Activity #23: Values Success Scrapbook

You're doing such a great job, kid! It's important to remember and celebrate all the times you acted according to your values.

What you will need:

You might want to ask an adult for help collecting these materials.

- pieces of colored paper, a scrapbook, or a blank notebook
- old magazines, newspapers, or printed pictures
- scissors (ask an adult for help)
- crayons, markers, or colored pencils
- glue or tape
- stickers or other decorations (optional)

1. **Find a comfortable spot.** This could be at the kitchen table, on the floor, or in your room.

2. **Let the decorating begin:** If you're using a blank notebook, start by decorating the cover. Write **"Values Success Scrapbook"** on the front and add your name. Use crayons, markers, stickers, and other decorations to make it special.

3. **Think about the values that are important to you**, such as kindness, honesty, bravery, creativity, respect, responsibility, friendship, patience, gratitude, politeness, and others.

4. Look through old magazines, newspapers, or printed pictures for images representing the times you acted according to your values. You can also draw your own pictures if you can't find any!

5. **On each page of your scrapbook, focus on ONE value.** Glue or tape pictures that represent actions you took based on that value. For example, if you have a page for kindness, you might paste a picture of you helping a friend, or you might draw sharing your toys with someone.

Write a few sentences next to each picture or drawing **about what you did and how it felt**.

For example, "I shared my toys with Louis today. It felt great to be kind, and I had a lot of fun, too!"

Important: This activity is a work in progress kind of thing. Every time you put a value into action, add it to your scrapbook. Over time, your scrapbook will become a wonderful collection of your successes!

FREE GUIDE: Mental Health Boosters for Kids

FREE DOWNLOAD ALERT!

Fun and Engaging Activities to Manage Your Children's Emotional Well-Being

https://barretthuang.com/mental-health-boosters/

Or scan the code below:

Kindness, Compassion, and Empathy

Tibby and Zip walked to a nearby park one sunny morning to play. As they passed by their neighbor Mrs. Whiskers' house, they noticed her struggling to carry a big bag of groceries up the steps.

"Let's help her, Zip!" Tibby said, and they both ran over to Mrs. Whiskers.

"Can we help you carry your groceries, Mrs. Whiskers?" Tibby asked with a big smile.

"Oh, thank you, dears! That would be wonderful," Mrs. Whiskers replied, looking relieved.

Tibby and Zip each took a handle of the heavy grocery bag and helped Mrs. Whiskers carry it into her house. After setting it down on the kitchen counter, Mrs. Whiskers gave them a warm hug.

"You two are so kind and thoughtful," she said. "Thank you for helping me."

As Tibby and Zip continued their walk to the park, they felt really happy and proud of themselves. They realized how good it felt to be kind and helpful to others.

Suddenly, Zip asked, "Tibby, why do I feel so happy?" "Kindness and compassion make the world a better place, Zip," Tibby said with a gentle smile.

Zip nodded. "So, by helping Mrs. Whiskers and making her feel good, we feel good too!"

"Exactly, dear Zip. Exactly," said Tibby.

What is Kindness and Compassion?

Kindness means being friendly and thoughtful of other people. It's about doing nice things for others and making them feel good.

Compassion means feeling concerned for others when they are sad or having a hard time. It's about wanting to help and make them feel better.

What's Empathy?

Empathy means trying to understand how someone else feels and sharing their feelings. It's like putting yourself in their shoes and caring about their emotions.

For example, when Tibby and Zip saw Mrs. Whiskers struggling to carry a big bag of groceries up the steps, this is what these values might look like:

Compassion: Zip, I'm concerned about Mrs. Whiskers. I don't want her to slip on the stairs and hurt herself.
Empathy: Oh, Mrs. Whiskers looks like she's struggling. Imagine trying to carry something so heavy when you're not so young anymore, and your bones hurt!
Kindness (in action): Oh, Mrs. Whiskers, please let us help you!

Kindness, compassion, and empathy are all very important values, not only because they make you feel good but also because they make the people you show these values happy! Simply put, these values make the world a better place for everyone.

Fun Activity #24: Kindness Game Board

Ready to play? I bet you are. Let's go!

Here are the game instructions:

1. Each day you will have a kindness challenge to complete. Ask your Mom or Dad (or an adult) for a die and a game piece (any will do). Every morning, roll the die and then move your game piece forward the corresponding number of spaces.

    For example, if the die shows four, you must move your game piece four spaces.

2. When you land on a space, read the kindness challenge written there. You have one whole day to complete this challenge.

    If you complete it, you can mark it off by putting a checkmark, crossing it out, or even putting a sticker on it.

    If you don't complete it, stay in that space until you do! This means you cannot roll the die the next day and move forward in the game.

3. Continue playing until you reach the "Finish" space. Celebrate your accomplishment by looking back at all the kindness challenges you completed!

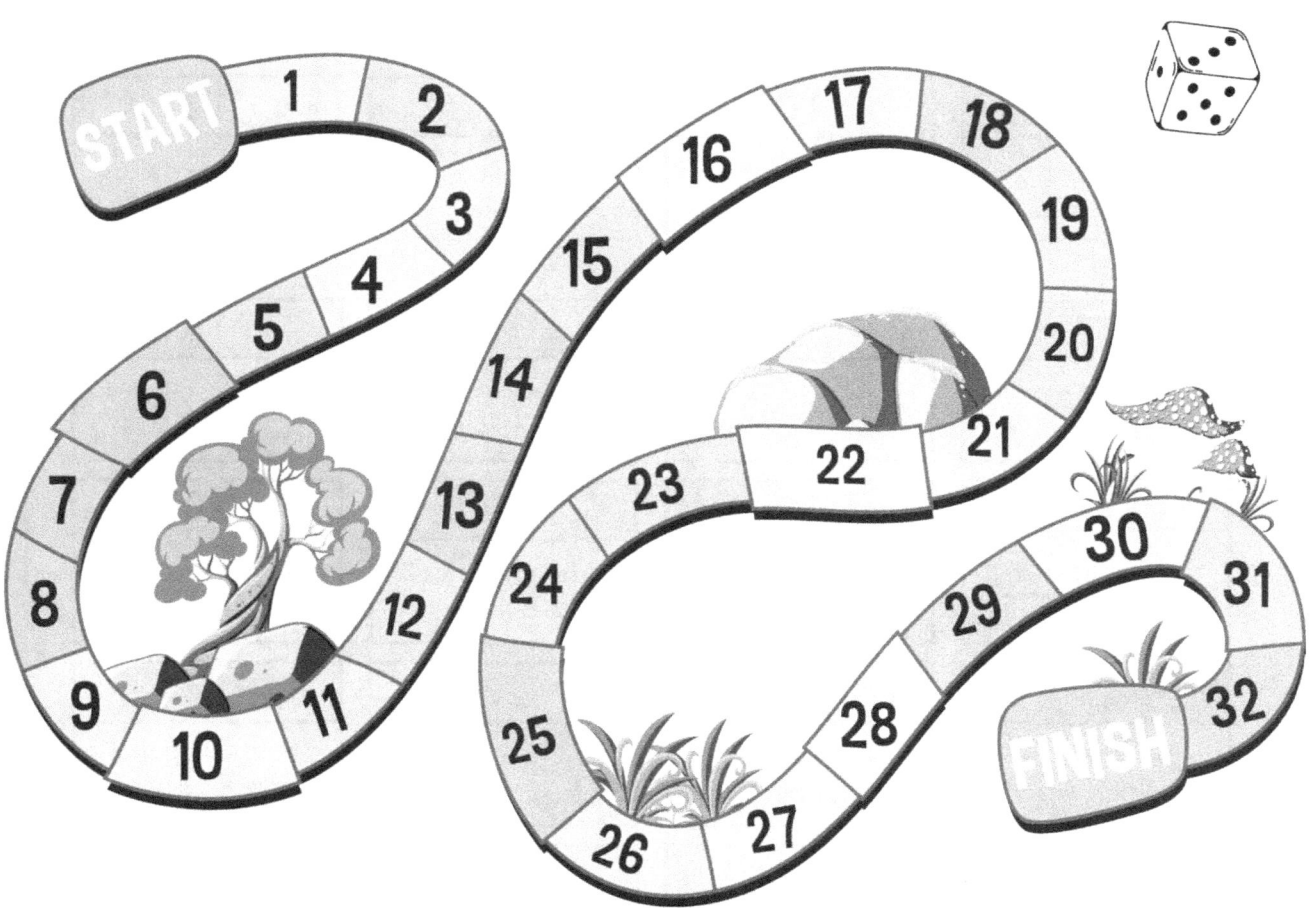

1	2	3	4
Pick up some litter at shcool	Hold the door open for others.	Include someone NEW when playing.	Do something nice for an adult.
5	**6**	**7**	**8**
Do something nice for a classmate.	Smile at people who pass you.	Do something nice for yourself.	Say Thank You to someone today.
9	**10**	**11**	**12**
Offer to help someone.	Give someone a hug.	Make someone smile.	Let someone know why you love them.
13	**14**	**15**	**16**
Offer to complete a chore.	Share something with a classmate.	Compliment someone.	Think of someone you need to say "Sorry" to and do it.
17	**18**	**19**	**20**
Collect some stuff you dont use and ask an adult to donate them for you	Fix your bed.	Listen attentively to a friend.	Use some of your pocket money and buy something for someone.
21	**22**	**23**	**24**
Offer your seat to another person.	Make someone laugh.	Be proactive and help others out.	Help set up the table for dinner.
25	**26**	**27**	**28**
Draw a picture for someone.	Help wash the dishes after a meal.	Thank a teacher.	Thank your parents / guardians.
29	**30**	**31**	**32**
Ask your mom or dad what you can do for them.	Don't play any online or video game and spend time with family.	Clean up your bedroom.	Ask someone how they feel.

Cool idea, alert! Play this game with one of your siblings or a friend and see who reaches the Finish line first! You'll need to use another game piece, but you should still only use one die.

- Place all the game pieces in the "Start" space.
- Decide who goes first by rolling the die. The player with the highest number goes first. (This is Player 1.)
- Player 1's Turn:
  - Player 1 rolls the die and moves their game piece forward the corresponding number of spaces.
  - Player 1 reads the kindness challenge on the space and must complete it on the same day. If they complete it, they can mark it off by putting a checkmark, crossing it out, or even putting a sticker on it. If they don't complete it, they stay in the space.
- Player 2's Turn:
  - Player 2 rolls the die the next day and moves their game piece forward with the corresponding number of spaces.
  - Player 2 reads the kindness challenge on the space and must complete it on the same day. If they complete it, they can mark it off by putting a checkmark, crossing it out, or even putting a sticker on it. If they don't complete it, they stay in the space.
- On Day 2, Player 1:
  - If they completed yesterday's kindness challenge, they roll the die and move their game piece forward with the corresponding number of spaces.
  - If they didn't complete yesterday's kindness challenge, they must do it today. (They don't roll the die today.)
- On Day 2, Player 2:
  - If they completed yesterday's kindness challenge, they roll the die and move their game piece forward with the corresponding number of spaces.

- If they didn't complete yesterday's kindness challenge, they must do it today. (They don't roll the die today.)

- Continue playing, taking turns each day, and completing kindness challenges. The first player to reach the "Finish" space after completing their final kindness challenge wins!

Fun Activity #25: Amazing Friendships

This activity will help you understand what makes a great friend and how you can be one!

1. **Find a comfortable spot.** This could be at the kitchen table, in your room, or even outside in a peaceful spot.

2. **Think about the friends you have** (or want to have). What can a friend do to make you feel happy or special? Here are some ideas to get you started:

   - A friend listens to me.
   - A friend likes to play and have lots of fun with me.
   - A friend helps me when I need it.
   - A friend doesn't lie to me.
   - A friend makes me laugh (not sad).
   - A friend apologizes when they make a mistake.

3. **Write everything you think** would make a good friend on the following page. You can use your crayons, markers, or colored pencils to make it colorful and fun.

4. When you're done, **look at what you wrote** and ask yourself if you're an example of what you think a good friend is.

   For example, if you wrote, "A friend listens to me," try remembering the last time you spent time with a friend and listened to them. If you can't remember such a time, you should reach out to a friend now and make it happen!

Fun Activity #26: Patience, Patience

Patience is not just "waiting"; it's waiting calmly without getting mad, upset, or whining. Being patient is part of being kind—to yourself and other people.

If you're patient, you can work hard and not give up, even when things take time. If you're patient with others, you understand and respect others' feelings and time (because you're not demanding their attention).

What you will need:
A watch or timer

1. **Find a comfortable spot.** This could be at the kitchen table, in your room, or even outside in a peaceful spot.

2. Think about times when you need to be patient. Here are some examples:
   - waiting for your birthday or a special event
   - waiting in line
   - waiting for a friend to finish talking
   - working on a difficult puzzle or project
   - waiting for your turn in a game or on the school playground

These are the three things I remember when I needed to be patient:

Situation #1: _____

Situation #2: _____

Situation #3: _____

3. Now, if you can go back in time, think and write down some ways you could have practiced more patience in any of the above situations.

Situation	Practice Patience by:
Example: *Waiting for my turn on the slide at the school playground*	*Example:* *Count to 10 slowly.* *Think about something happy or fun.*

4. Practice patience for a certain amount of time using your watch or a timer. For example, sit on a chair and set your watch or a timer for 5 minutes. Next, practice waiting calmly without getting upset by counting slowly or taking deep breaths.

Don't check your watch or look at the timer. Patiently wait until the time's up. This way, the next time you need to wait, you'll be a lot more patient than you were before!

Staying Healthy and Happy

Tibby and Zip are done playing in their room and are having a snack. After taking a single bite of an apple, Zip reached into a bag and pulled out a big stash of snacks. He started munching on cookies, chips, and candy all at once. Tibby watched with concern.

"Zip, I think you're eating too many snacks," Tibby said gently.
"Eating too much junk food isn't good for you."

Zip stopped mid-bite and looked at Tibby.
"But they taste so good! Why isn't it good to eat
a lot of them?"

"Well," Tibby began, "eating too much junk food can make you feel tired and sick. It doesn't give you the energy and nutrients you need to play and grow. We need to eat healthy foods to stay strong and happy."

"So, what should I eat instead?" Zip asked, slightly annoyed.

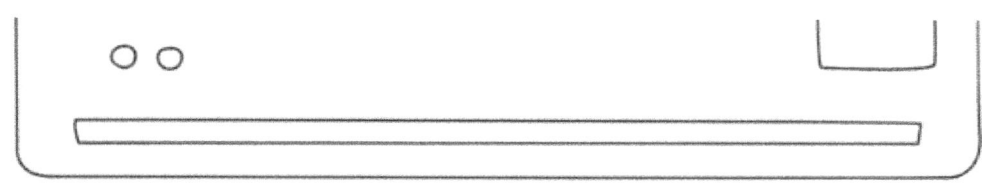

"How about some fruits and nuts?" Tibby suggested, handing Zip his forgotten apple and a handful of almonds. "They're delicious and good for you."

Zip smiled and took another bite of the apple. "An apple IS pretty tasty. Thanks, Tibby."

"You're welcome, Zip!" Tibby said. "And there's another thing we should talk about—balancing screen time. It's important to limit how much time we spend on screens like tablets, phones, and TV."

"Why is that?" Zip asked, curious.

"Too much screen time can make us tired and even hurt our eyes," Tibby explained.

"Plus, when we spend too much time on screens, we miss out on fun activities like playing outside, reading, or spending time with friends and family," Tibby said.

"Okay, but I really do like playing video games too..." Zip wondered.

"Let's make sure we have a good balance," Tibby suggested. "For every hour of screen time, we can spend an hour playing outside, reading, or doing something creative!"

Zip nodded enthusiastically. "That sounds like a great plan, Tibby!"

How to Develop Good Habits to Be Amazing Kids

Kids, it's important to learn how to stay healthy and happy. The way to do this is to make sure you take care of your body and mind to be the best you can be.

Here are some ideas to be healthy and happy:

- **Eat Nutritious Foods.** Eating healthy foods gives you the energy you need to play, learn, and grow. Make sure to eat lots of fruits and vegetables!

- **Get Enough Sleep.** Sleep is super important for your body and mind. It helps you feel rested and ready for the day. So, try to go to bed at the same time every night (8:00 or 9:00 PM) and wake up at the same time every morning (6:00 or 7:00 AM).

- **Balance Your Screen Time.** It's important to limit screen time (e.g., watching TV, playing video games, etc.) and balance it with other activities. Just like Tibby and Zip, try this: For every hour of screen time, spend an hour playing outside, reading, or doing something creative!

- **Take Care of Your Body.** Exercise keeps your body healthy and strong. Find activities you enjoy, like running, biking, swimming, or playing sports, and do them regularly.

- **Take Care of Your Mind.** Just like your body, your mind needs care too. Practice mindfulness (like the exercises in [Chapter 2: What Mindfulness Means](#)), read books, play games that challenge your brain (like doing a puzzle), and make sure you talk about your feelings with someone you trust whenever you're sad, worried or feel overwhelmed (like one of your [Safe People](#), page 38).

Let's keep exploring how to say healthy and happy with the exercises below!

Fun Activity #27: High Five to Healthy Habits

In the High Five to Healthy Habits diagram below, write down at least TWO healthy habits you want to do for each category. Here are some ideas for you:

Category: Sleep & Rest
- ☐ Go to bed at the same time every night.
- ☐ Keep your bedroom dark and quiet for sleep.
- ☐ Wake up at the same time every morning.
- ☐ Take a nap when feeling tired.
- ☐ Avoid screen time an hour before bed.

Category: Food & Nutrition
- ☐ Eat breakfast every morning.
- ☐ Eat at least one fruit every day.
- ☐ Drink plenty of water (e.g., 8 glasses) throughout the day.
- ☐ Include vegetables in every meal.
- ☐ Choose one day when you don't eat any unhealthy or sugar-y drink (e.g., soda) or snack (e.g., cookie, chips, etc.)

Category: Relationships & Emotions
- ☐ Share toys and play with friends.
- ☐ Spend time talking with family members.
- ☐ Practice saying "please" and "thank you."
- ☐ Listen carefully when others are speaking.
- ☐ Offer help to someone in need.

Category: Exercise & Movement
- ☐ Play outside for at least 30 minutes a day.
- ☐ Join a sports team or physical activity group.
- ☐ Take the stairs instead of the elevator.
- ☐ Dance to your favorite music.
- ☐ Ride your bike around the neighborhood.

Category: Playing & Creativity
- ☐ Draw or paint a picture.
- ☐ Build something with blocks or Legos.
- ☐ Play a musical instrument.
- ☐ Create a story and act it out.
- ☐ Spend time on a hobby like cooking (with adult supervision) or model building.

BONUS Healthy Habits:
- ☐ Brush your teeth twice a day.
- ☐ Keep your room clean and organized.
- ☐ Wash your hands before eating and after using the bathroom.
- ☐ Practice deep breathing exercises.
- ☐ Spend time in nature, like visiting a park with your parents.

High Five to Healthy Habits

Relationships & Emotions

Food & Nutrition

Exercise & Movement

Sleep & Rest

Playing & Creativity

Fun Activity #28: Writing a Letter to a Friend or Family Member

Whatever your thoughts or feelings, it's good to know how to share them with someone special. Let's get started!

What you will need:

- a piece of paper or a blank card
- an envelope (optional)
- a pen, pencil, or markers
- stickers or drawings (optional for decoration)

1. **Find a comfortable spot.** This could be at the kitchen table, on the floor, or in your room.

2. **Think about someone special.** Who do you want to write to? It could be a friend, a family member, or teacher. Imagine their smiling face and think about why they are special to you.

3. At the top of your paper, write a friendly greeting. Here are some examples:

    - Dear Grandma,
    - Hi Emma,
    - Hello Uncle John,
    - Dear Mom/Dad,

4. Next, write about what you've been thinking and feeling. Here are some ideas to get you started:

    - **Talk about your day**: "Today, I had so much fun playing at the park with my friends."

- **Share something you're excited about**: "I'm really looking forward to my birthday party next week!"
- **Express your feelings**: "I felt a little sad yesterday because I missed you."
- **Ask how they are doing**: "How have you been? I hope you're doing well."
- **Include a Special Memory**: Write about a special memory you have with this person. It could be a fun trip you took together, a game you played, or a time they helped you with something. For example, "Remember when we went to the beach last summer? I had so much fun building sandcastles with you."
- **Ask a Question**: A question is a great way to keep the conversation going. It shows that you're interested in hearing back from them. For example, ask, "What have you been up to lately?" or "Do you have any fun plans for the weekend?"

5. Finish your letter with a warm closing and your name. Here are some examples:

- Love, Sarah
- Your friend, Max
- Hugs, Lily

6. If you like, you can decorate your letter with drawings, stickers, or colorful doodles. Make it as bright and fun as you want!

7. Give your letter to the person you wrote it to. Ask an adult to help you mail your letter if they live far away. If they live nearby, you can hand it to them yourself.

Here's an example letter using all the tips above:

Dear Grandma,

Today, I had so much fun playing at the park with my friends. We played on the swings and had a picnic. But, I felt a little sad yesterday too because I missed you. How have you been? I hope you're doing well.

Remember when we went to the park last summer at your place? I had so much running around while you and Grandpa were walking behind me.

Anyway, will you be visiting soon? I'm sure Mom and Dad miss you and Grandpa too.

Love,
Sarah

It's your turn to write your letter! If you need any help, be sure to ask your Mom or Dad, your teacher, or any adult you trust.

_____
_____
_____
_____
_____
_____
_____
_____
_____
_____
_____
_____
_____
_____
_____
_____
_____

No-Screen Fun Stuff

This activity will help you find many fun things to do without using screens like TVs, tablets, or phones. Let's get started!

1. **Find a comfortable spot.** This could be at the kitchen table, in your room, or even outside in a peaceful spot.

2. Think about all the fun things you can do without using a screen. Here are some cool ideas from Tibby and Zip! Go ahead and put a checkmark next to the non-screen activities you like.

- ☐ **Play outside**: Run, skip, hop, or jump in the yard or park.
- ☐ **Ride a bike**: Enjoy a fun ride around your neighborhood.
- ☐ **Read a book**: Pick a book and dive into an exciting story.
- ☐ **Draw or paint a picture**: Let your creativity flow with some art.
- ☐ **Build with Legos or blocks**: Create buildings, cars, or anything you can imagine.
- ☐ **Play a board game**: Enjoy a fun game with family or friends.
- ☐ **Do a puzzle**: Challenge yourself with a jigsaw puzzle.
- ☐ **Make something artsy**: Create something cool with paper, glue, and other craft supplies.
- ☐ **Bake cookies with an adult**: Enjoy the process and the tasty results!
- ☐ **Have a picnic**: Pack a meal and eat outside in a park or backyard. You can do this with your parents or caregiver, your siblings if you have any, your friends, or you can just have fun alone.
- ☐ **Go on a nature walk with an adult**: Explore a local trail or park and observe the plants and animals.
- ☐ **Play with a pet**: Spend time caring for and playing with your pet.
- ☐ **Write a story**: Use your imagination to create a short story.
- ☐ **Sing and dance to your favorite songs**: Have a mini dance party.

- ☐ **Help with chores around the house**: Clean your room, help with laundry, or set the table.
- ☐ **Play hide and seek**: Have fun hiding and finding friends or family members.
- ☐ **Build a fort with blankets and pillows**: Create a cozy hideout.
- ☐ **Do a science experiment with an adult**: Try simple experiments like making a volcano or growing crystals.
- ☐ **Write a letter to a friend or family member**: Share your thoughts and feelings in a letter.
- ☐ **Make homemade playdough**: Create and play with your own colorful dough.
- ☐ **Fly a kite**: Go to an open space and enjoy flying a kite with an adult.
- ☐ **Go fishing**: Spend a peaceful day fishing with an adult.
- ☐ **Practice yoga**: Stretch and relax with some simple yoga poses for kids.
- ☐ **Learn a new sport**: Try playing soccer, basketball, or another sport.
- ☐ **Go to a playground**: Swing, slide, and climb at a local playground.
- ☐ **Make a scrapbook**: Collect photos and memories to create a scrapbook.
- ☐ **Paint rocks**: Find some smooth rocks and paint them with fun designs.
- ☐ **Visit a museum with an adult**: Explore exhibits and learn something new.
- ☐ **Build a sandcastle with an adult**: If you're near a beach or sandbox, create an amazing sandcastle.
- ☐ **Make friendship bracelets**: Create colorful bracelets to share with friends.
- ☐ **Learn to cook a simple meal with an adult**: Help in the kitchen and learn to cook something easy.
- ☐ **Visit a library**: Explore and check out new books to read.
- ☐ **Go on a bug hunt**: Explore your yard and see what insects you can find.
- ☐ **Make a time capsule**: Collect items and memories to open in the future.
- ☐ **Create a photo album**: Organize and decorate a photo album.
- ☐ **Make a music playlist**: Put together your favorite songs to listen to later.
- ☐ **Make a vision board**: Cut out pictures and words from magazines that inspire you.
- ☐ **Learn magic tricks**: Practice and perform magic tricks for your family and friends.
- ☐ **Got any other ideas? Write them here!**

_____
_____
_____
_____

3. **Be sure to pick at least one no-screen activity every day.** Choose one or more activities from the list above, or create your own. Try to do different activities each day to keep things exciting and fun!

Day	No-Screen Activity
Example: *Day 1*	*Example:* *Fly a kite*
Day 1	
Day 2	
Day 3	
Day 4	
Day 5	
Day 6	
Day 7	

Conclusion

Hi, kids. You've done an amazing job
learning and doing all the exercises in this
Acceptance and Commitment Therapy (ACT) book.
Good job! You should be really proud of yourself.
Tibby and Zip sure are!

ACT is a superpower! It gives you important skills to manage your thoughts and feelings, especially the really tough ones. For example, if you think you can't do something, that might be a difficult thought to have because it makes you unsure and less confident. If you feel angry or sad, those might be tough feelings to have because they might make you say or do something you don't want.

Luckily, with the skills in this book, you can handle tough thoughts and feelings like these! So, here's a really quick review of what you learned.

Important: Before we do our review, it's important to know that if there's anything at all that's confusing to you, please ask an adult to help you figure things out. It can be your parents, an older sibling, a teacher, or any adult you trust and feel comfortable talking to. Okay, here's our recap!

In Chapter 1. Understanding Your Feelings, you learned about all the different emotions you can have and how to understand them better.

- Fun Activity #1: Today I Feel: You created a chart to express how you feel each day.
- Fun Activity #2: Feelings Diary: You wrote about your feelings in a diary.
- Fun Activity #3: Safe People: You identified safe people you can talk to about your feelings.
- Fun Activity #4: Feelings and Body Map: You mapped out where you feel different emotions in your body.

In Chapter 2. What Mindfulness Means, you explored mindfulness and how it helps you stay calm and focused.

- Fun Activity #5: Mindful Breathing: You practiced deep breathing to feel calm.

- Fun Activity #6: Mindful Listening: You listened to the sounds around you to improve focus.
- Fun Activity #7: Mindful Eating: You paid attention to the taste and texture of your food.
- Fun Activity #8: Mindfulness Jar: You created a jar to watch how glitter settles, just like your feelings.
- Fun Activity #9: Mindful Coloring: You colored mindfully to relax and focus.

In Chapter 3. Acceptance and Letting Go, you learned about accepting your feelings and letting go of the ones that bother, stress, or overwhelm you.

- Fun Activity #10: Balloon Release: You let go of difficult feelings by imagining them floating away in a balloon.
- Fun Activity #11: The Worry Box: You wrote down your worries and put them in a box to help let them go.
- Fun Activity #12: I'm a Good Kid: You wrote positive affirmations to remind yourself of your good qualities.

In Chapter 4. Learning About Your Thoughts, you explored how to understand and manage your thoughts. You learned that thoughts are not permanent; they come and go. You also learned that you shouldn't let unhelpful or negative thoughts get the better of you.

- Fun Activity #13: Thought Bubbles: You wrote your thoughts in bubbles to see them more clearly.
- Fun Activity #14: Thought Train: You imagined your thoughts as a train passing by.
- Fun Activity #15: Clouds in the Sky: You watched your thoughts float by like clouds.
- Fun Activity #16: Mountain Meditation: You imagined being a strong and mighty mountain to help you stay calm when you're having negative thoughts.

- Fun Activity #17: Thought Untangling Cards: You used fun cards to help you deal with bad or negative thoughts. By using a playful element to these thoughts, you lessened their power over you!

In Chapter 5. Knowing What Matters, you discovered what you like or what's important to you (values).

- Fun Activity #18: Values BINGO: You played BINGO to identify your values.
- Fun Activity #19: Likes and Dislikes: You explored what you like and dislike to understand your values.
- Fun Activity #20: It's My Birthday! It's My Birthday!: You imagined your ideal birthday to find out what matters to you.

In Chapter 6, Doing What Matters, you learned how to behave (act) according to your values.

- Fun Activity #21: Doing What Matters Schedule: You created a schedule based on your values.
- Fun Activity #22: I'm a SMART Kid: You set SMART goals to achieve what matters to you.
- Fun Activity #23: W.O.O.P. Your Goal!: You used the WOOP technique to plan and achieve your goals.
- Fun Activity #24: Values Success Scrapbook: You made a scrapbook of your achievements based on your values.

In Chapter 7. Kindness, Compassion, and Empathy, you explored how to be kind, compassionate, and empathetic.

- Fun Activity #25: Kindness Game Board: You played a game to practice acts of kindness.
- Fun Activity #26: Amazing Friendships: You learned what you like in a friend and how to be a good friend.
- Fun Activity #27: Patience, Patience: You practiced being patient and understanding.

In Chapter 8, Staying Healthy and Happy, you learned about habits that keep you healthy and happy!

- Fun Activity #28: High Five to Healthy Habits: You identified healthy habits in five different areas.
- Fun Activity #29: Writing a Letter to a Friend or Family Member: You learned how to share your thoughts and feelings in a letter.
- Fun Activity #30: No-Screen Fun Stuff: You explored fun activities to do without screens!

Being a kid is super fun, but it's not always fun and games. Sometimes, you feel unhelpful and powerful emotions, and sometimes you get negative or harmful thoughts. But you know what? EVERYONE experiences these. Adults too!

So, what's the secret to being a happy and healthy kid?

According to ACT, and Tibby and Zip, these are the secrets:

Secret #1: Learn how to manage your thoughts and emotions. Remember, you're the boss, so you have control over your feelings and thoughts.

Secret #2: Know your likes and what's important to you (values).

Secret #3: Make decisions or behave according to your values.

Sprinkle the above secrets with the staying healthy and happy tips in this book (Chapter 8), and not only will you be an amazing kid, but you'll also be an amazing adult in the future!

FREE GUIDE: Mental Health Boosters for Kids

FREE DOWNLOAD ALERT!

Fun and Engaging Activities to Manage Your Children's Emotional Well-Being

https://barretthuang.com/mental-health-boosters/

Or scan the code below:

Review Request

If you enjoyed this book or found it useful…

I'd like to ask you for a quick favor:

Please share your thoughts and **leave a quick REVIEW**. Your feedback matters and helps me make improvements to provide the best books possible.

Reviews are so helpful to both readers and authors, so any help would be greatly appreciated.

You can leave a review here:

https://tinyurl.com/act-kids-review

Or by scanning the QR code below:

Also, please join my ARC team to get early access to my releases.

https://barretthuang.com/arc-team/

Further Reading

DBT Workbook for Kids

Fun & Practical Dialectal Behavior Therapy Skills Training For Children

Help Kids Recognize Their Emotions, Manage Anxiety & Phobias, and Learn To Thrive!

Get your copy here:

https://tinyurl.com/dbtkids

Boundaries Workbook for Kids

Fun, Educational & Age-Appropriate Lessons About Personal Safety & Consent

Learn to Set Healthy Body Boundaries at Home, School, & Online

(For Ages 8-12)

Get your copy here:

https://tinyurl.com/Boundaries-Workbook-for-Kids

DBT Workbook For Teens

A Complete Dialectical Behavior Therapy Toolkit

Essential Coping Skills and Practical Activities To Help Teenagers & Adolescents Manage Stress, Anxiety, ADHD, Phobias & More

Get your copy here:

https://tinyurl.com/dbt-teens

About the Author

Barrett Huang is an author and businessman. Barrett spent years discovering the best ways to manage his OCD, overcome his anxiety, and learn to embrace life. Through his writing, he hopes to share his knowledge with readers, empowering people of all backgrounds with the tools and strategies they need to improve their mental wellbeing and be happy and healthy.

When not writing or running his business, Barrett loves to spend his time studying. He has majored in psychology and completed the DBT skills certificate course by Dr. Marsha Linehan. Barrett's idol is Bruce Lee, who said, "The key to immortality is first living a life worth remembering."

https://barretthuang.com/